Copyright © 2011
All rights reserved.
Printed in the United States of America

Third Edition

The contents of this book are the property of Brown Technical Publications Inc. All rights reserved. No part of this book covered by the copyright hereon may be reproduced or used in any form or by any means, electronic or mechanical, including photocopying, recording, or by any information storage and retrieval system.

While every precaution has been taken in preparation of this book, the author and publisher assumes no responsibility for errors or omissions. Neither is any liability assumed from the use of the information contained herein. The reader is expressly warned to consider and adopt all safety precautions and to avoid all potential hazards. The publisher and author make no representations or warranties of any kind, nor are any such representations implied with respect to the material set forth here. The publisher and author shall not be liable for
any special, consequently, or exemplary damages resulting, in whole **or part, from the reader's use of, or reliance upon, this material.**

National Electrical Code® and the NEC® are registered Trademarks of the National Fire Protection Association, Inc., Quincy, MA

Author: Ray Holder

Copyright© 2016

CONTENTS

PREFACE..I
USEFUL FORMULAS.. VIII
EXAM #1 - MAINTENANCE ELECTRICIAN..1
EXAM #2 - MAINTENANCE ELECTRICAN...7
EXAM #3 - RESIDENTIAL ELECTRICIAN..14
EXAM #4 - RESIDENTIAL ELECTRICIAN..20
EXAM #5 - RESIDENTIAL ELECTRICIAN..26
EXAM #6 - RESIDENTIAL ELECTRICIAN..32
EXAM #7 - JOURNEYMAN ELECTRICIAN..38
EXAM #8 - JOURNEYMAN ELECTRICIAN..44
EXAM #9 - JOURNEYMAN ELECTRICIAN..50
EXAM #10 - JOURNEYMAN ELECTRICIAN..56

EXAM #11 - JOURNEYMAN ELECTRICIAN..62
EXAM #12 - MASTER ELECTRICIAN...68
EXAM #13 - MASTER ELECTRICIAN...74
EXAM #14 - MASTER ELECTRICIAN...81
EXAM #15 - MASTER ELECTRICIAN...88
EXAM #16 - MASTER ELECTRICIAN... 94

EXAM #17- SIGN ELECTRICIAN...101

EXAM #18- SIGN ELECTRICIAN………………………………………....107

FINAL EXAM - RESIDENTIAL ELECTRICIAN.......................................115

Copyright© 2016

FINAL EXAM - JOURNEYMAN ELECTRICIAN..133
FINAL EXAM - MASTER ELECTRICIAN..151
ANSWER KEY EXAM #1..176
ANSWER KEY EXAM #2..178
ANSWER KEY EXAM #3..180
ANSWER KEY EXAM #4..182
ANSWER KEY EXAM #5..184
ANSWER KEY EXAM #6..186
ANSWER KEY EXAM #7..188
ANSWER KEY EXAM #8..190
ANSWER KEY EXAM #9..192
ANSWER KEY EXAM #10..194
ANSWER KEY EXAM #11..196
ANSWER KEY EXAM #12..198
ANSWER KEY EXAM #13..200
ANSWER KEY EXAM #14..203
ANSWER KEY EXAM #15..206
ANSWER KEY EXAM #16..208
ANSWER KEY EXAM#17...210
ANSWER KEY EXAM #18..212
ANSWER KEY - RESIDENTIAL ELECTRICIAN FINAL EXAM...........................214
ANSWER KEY - JOURNEYMAN ELECTRICIAN FINAL EXAM..........................218
ANSWER KEY - MASTER ELECTRICIAN FINAL EXAM....................................223

PREFACE

HOW TO PREPARE FOR THE EXAM

This book is a guide to preparing for the electricians' licensing exam. It will not make you a competent electrician, nor teach you the electrical trade, but it will give you an idea of the type of questions asked on most electricians' licensing examinations and how to answer them correctly.

Most electrical exams consist of multiple-choice questions and this is the type of questions reflected in this exam guide. These questions will give you a feel for how many of the examinations nationwide are structured. These questions are an example of the many questions the author has encountered when taking numerous exams in recent years.

Begin your pre-exam preparation with two points in mind.
   Opportunities in life will arise - be prepared for them.
   The more you LEARN - the more you EARN.

Attempting to take an exam without preparation is a complete waste of time. Attend classes at your local community college. Attend seminars, electrical code updates, and company sponsored programs. Many major electrical suppliers and local unions sponsor classes of this type at no cost. Take advantage of them.

Become familiar with the National Electrical Code®; the Code has a LANGUAGE all its own. Understanding this language will help you to better interpret the NEC®. Do not become intimidated by its length. Become thoroughly familiar with the definitions in Chapter One; if you don't, the remainder of the NEC® will be difficult to comprehend. Remember, on the job we use different "lingo" and phrases compared to the way the NEC® is written and to the way many test questions are expressed.

HOW TO STUDY

Before beginning to study, get into the right frame of mind, and relax. Study in a quiet place that is conducive to learning. If such a place is not available, go to your local library. It is important that you have the right atmosphere in which to study.

It is much better to study many short lengths of time than attempt to study fewer, longer lengths of time. Try to study a little while, say about an hour, every evening. You will need the support and understanding of your family to set aside this much needed time.

As you study this exam preparation book, the NEC® and other references, always highlight the important points. This makes it easier to locate Code references when taking the exam.

Copyright© 2016

Use a straight edge, such as a six-inch ruler when using the NEC® tables and charts. A very common mistake is to get on the wrong line when using these tables; when that happens, the result is an incorrect answer.

Use tabs on the major sections of your NEC®, so they are faster and easier to locate when taking the exam. The national average allowed per question is less than three minutes, you cannot waste time.

WHAT TO STUDY

A common reason for one to be unsuccessful when attempting to pass electrical exams is not knowing what to study. Approximately forty percent of most exams are known as "core" questions. These type of questions are reflected in this exam preparation book.

The subject matter covered in most electrical license examinations is:

0 Grounding and bonding
1 Overcurrent protection
2 Wiring methods and installation
3 Boxes and fittings
4 Services and equipment
5 Motors
6 Special occupancies
7 Load calculations
8 Lighting
9 Appliances
10 Box and raceway fill
11 Hazardous locations

Become very familiar with questions on the above. Knowing what to study is a major step toward passing your exam.

HELPFUL HINTS ON TAKING THE EXAM

0 **Complete the easy questions first.** On most tests, all questions are valued the same. If you become too frustrated on any one question, it may reflect upon your entire test.

1 **Keep track of time.** Do not spend too much time on one question. If a question is difficult for you, mark the answer sheet the answer you think is correct and place a check (✓) by that question in the examination booklet. Then go on to the next question; if you have time after finishing the rest of the exam, you can go back to the questions you have checked. If you simply do not know the answer to a question, take a guess. Choose the answer that is most familiar to you. In most cases, the answer is B or C.

0 Only change answers if you know you are right. - Usually, your first answer is your best answer.

1 Relax - Do not get uptight and stressed out when testing.

2 Tab your Code Book. - References are easier and faster to find.

3 Use a straightedge. - Prevent getting on the wrong line when referring to the tables in the NEC®.

4 Get a good nights rest before the exam. - Do not attempt to drive several hours to an exam site; be rested and alert.

5 Understand the question. - One key word in a question can make a difference in what the question is asking. Underlining key words will help you to understand the meaning of the question.

6 Use a dependable calculator. - Use a solar-powered calculator that has a battery back-up. Since many test sites are not well lighted, this type of calculator will prepare you for such a situation. If possible, bring along a spare calculator.

7 Show up at least 30 minutes prior to your exam time. – Be sure to allow yourself time for traffic, etc. when planning your route to the exam location.

TYPICAL REGULATIONS AT THE PLACE OF EXAMINATION

To ensure that all examinees are examined under equally favorable conditions, the following regulations and procedures are observed at most examination sites:

5888 Each examinee must present proper photo identification, preferably your driver's license before you will be permitted to take the examination.

5889 No cameras, notes, tape recorders, pagers, or cellular phones are allowed in the examination room.

5890 No one will be permitted to work beyond the established time limits.

5891 Examinees are not permitted any reference material EXCEPT the National Electrical Code®.

5892 Examinees will be permitted to use noiseless calculators during the examination. Calculators which provide programmable ability or pre-programmed calculators are prohibited.

0 Permission of an examination proctor must be obtained before leaving the room while the examination is in progress.

1 Each examinee is assigned to a seat specifically designated by name and/or number when admitted to the examination room.

TYPICAL EXAMINATION QUESTIONS

The following examples are intended to illustrate typical questions that appear on electricians' licensing exams.

EXAMPLE 1

An equipment grounding conductor of a branch circuit shall be identified by which of the following colors?

23 gray
24 white
25 black
26 green

Here you are asked to select from the listed colors the one that is to be used to identify the equipment grounding conductor of a branch circuit. Since Section 250.119 of the NEC® requires that green or green with yellow stripes be the color of insulation used on a grounding conductor (when it is not bare), the answer is **D**.

EXAMPLE 2

A circuit leading to a gasoline dispensing pump must have a disconnecting means _____.

23 only in the grounded conductors
24 only in the ungrounded conductors
25 operating independently in all conductors
26 that simultaneously disconnects both the grounded and ungrounded conductors supplying the dispensing pump

Here the "question" is in the form of an incomplete statement. Your task is to select the choice that best completes the statement. In this case, you should have selected **D** since Section 514.11(A) of the NEC® specifies that such a circuit shall be provided with a means to disconnect simultaneously from the source of supply all conductors of a circuit, including the grounded conductor.

EXAMPLE 3

A building or other structure served shall be supplied by only one service EXCEPT one where the capacity requirements are in excess of _____.

23 800 amperes at a supply voltage of 600 volts or less
24 1000 amperes at a supply voltage of 600 volts or less
25 1500 amperes at a supply voltage of 600 volts or less
26 2000 amperes at a supply voltage of 600 volts or less

Again, the "question" is in the form of an incomplete statement and your task is to select the choice that best completes the statement. In this case, you are to find an exception. You have to select the condition that has to be met when supplying a building or structure by more than one service. You should have selected **D** because Section 230.2(C)(1) requires the conditions listed in **D** but does not require or permit the conditions listed in A, B, or C.

EXAMPLE 4

Disregarding exceptions, the MINIMUM size overhead service-drop conductor shall be _____ AWG copper.

23 6
24 8
25 12
26 14

Here the "question" is in the form of fill in the blank and your task is to select the choice that best completes the statement. In this case, exceptions are not applicable. You have to select the minimum size conductor required for overhead service-drop conductors. You should have selected **B** because Section 230.23(B) specifies that the conductors shall not be smaller than 8 AWG copper.

HOW TO USE THIS BOOK

Practice exams numbers 1-18 contained in this book consists of 25 questions each. The time allotted for each of these practice exams is 75 minutes or 3 minutes per question. The final exams vary in length depending on the level of test the student will be taking. The allotted time for each final exam is noted on the exam and also varies due to the level of testing. Using this time limit as a standard, you should be able to complete an actual examination in the allotted time. Each exam varies in difficulty depending upon the exam level.

To get the most out of this book you should answer every question and highlight your NEC® for future reference. If you have difficulty with a question and cannot come up with the answer that is familiar to you, put a check mark next to the question and come back to it after completing the remainder of the questions. Review your answers with the **ANSWER KEY** located in the back of this book. This will help you identify your strengths and weaknesses. When you discover you are weaker in some areas than others, you will know that further study is necessary in those areas.

Do only one practice exam contained in this book during an allotted study period. This way you do not get burned out and fatigued trying to study for too long a period of time. This also helps you develop good study habits. **GOOD LUCK!**

ABOUT THE AUTHOR

H. Ray Holder has worked in the electrical industry for over forty-five years as an apprentice, journeyman, master, field engineer, estimator, business manager, contractor, inspector, consultant, and instructor.

Mr. Holder is a graduate of Texas State University and holds a Bachelor of Science Degree in Occupational Education. He also holds a lifetime teaching certificate from the Texas Education Agency, in the field of Vocational Education.

He is a certified instructor of electrical trades. His classes are presented in a simplified, easy-to-understand format for electricians.

He has taught over 30,000 students at Austin Community College, and the University of Texas at Austin, Texas, Odessa College, at Odessa, Texas, Howard College at San Angelo, Texas, Technical-Vocational Institute of Albuquerque, New Mexico, and in the public school systems in Ft. Worth and San Antonio, Texas. He is currently the Director of Education for Electrical Seminars, Inc. of San Marcos, Texas.

Mr. Holder is an active member of the National Fire Protection Association, International Association of Electrical Inspectors, and retired member of the International Brotherhood of Electrical Workers.

OTHER TITLES AVAILABLE BASED ON THE 2011 NEC©

Practical Calculations for Electricians

Electricians Practice Calculations Exams

Texas Electricians Practice Exams & Study Guide

Electricians Handbook of NEC® Questions

USEFUL FORMULAS

To Find	Single Phase	Three Phase	Direct Current
Amperes when kVA is known	$\dfrac{kVA \times 1{,}000}{E}$	$\dfrac{kVA \times 1{,}000}{E \times 1.732}$	not applicable
Amperes when horsepower is known	$\dfrac{HP \times 746}{E \times \%Eff. \times PF.}$	$\dfrac{HP \times 746}{E \times 1.732 \times \%Eff. \times PF.}$	$\dfrac{HP \times 746}{E \times \%Eff.}$
Amperes when Kilowatts are known	$\dfrac{kW \times 1{,}000}{E \times PF.}$	$\dfrac{kW \times 1{,}000}{E \times 1.732 \times PF.}$	$\dfrac{kW \times 1{,}000}{E}$
Kilowatts	$\dfrac{I \times E \times PF.}{1{,}000}$	$\dfrac{I \times E \times 1.732 \times PF.}{1{,}000}$	$\dfrac{I \times E}{1{,}000}$
Kilovolt Amperes	$\dfrac{I \times E}{1{,}000}$	$\dfrac{I \times E \times 1.732}{1{,}000}$	not applicable
Horsepower	$\dfrac{I \times E \times \%Eff. \times PF.}{746}$	$\dfrac{I \times E \times 1.732 \times \%Eff. \times PF.}{746}$	$\dfrac{I \times E \times \%Eff.}{746}$
Watts	$E \times I \times PF.$	$E \times I \times 1.732 \times PF.$	$E \times I$

I = Amperes

E = Volt

kW = Kilowatts

kVA = Kilovolt-Amperes

HP = Horsepower

%Eff. = Percent Efficiency

PF. = Power Factor

Copyright© 2016

Power – "Pie" Circle Formulas

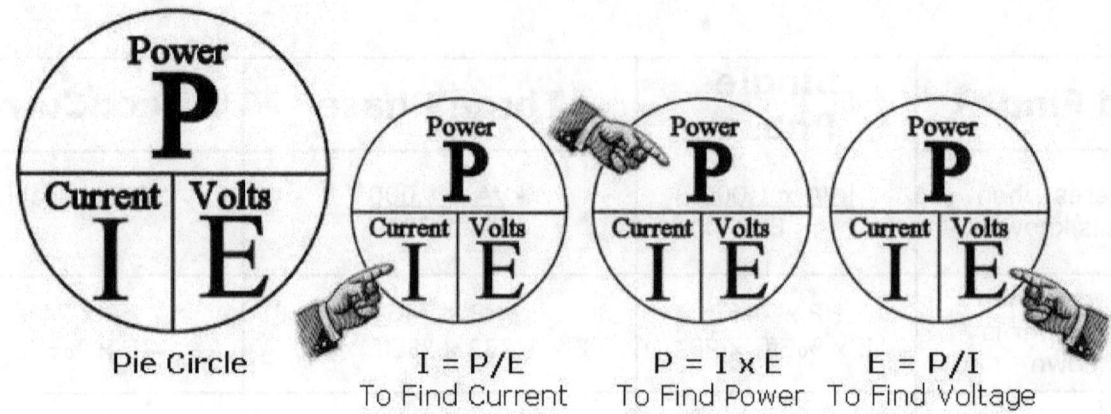

Ohms Law Circle Formulas

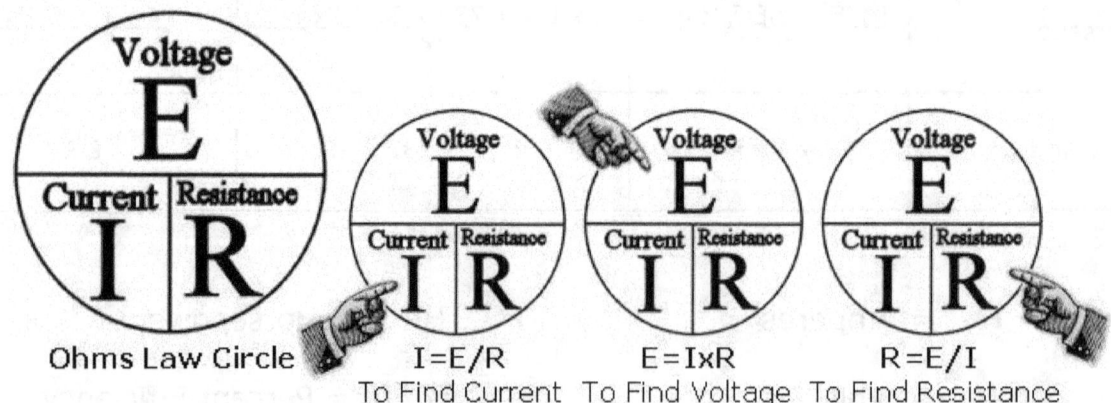

Copyright© 2016

Power Factor Triangle Formulas

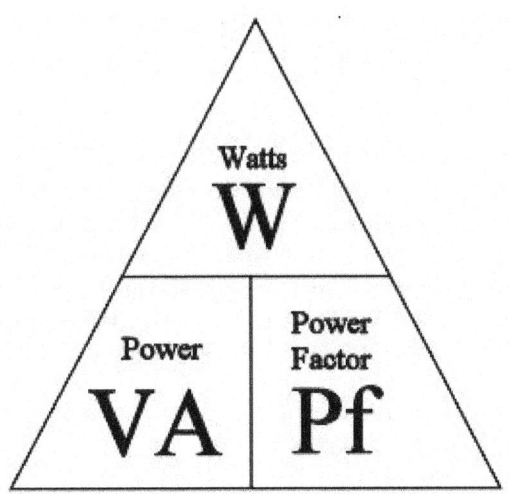

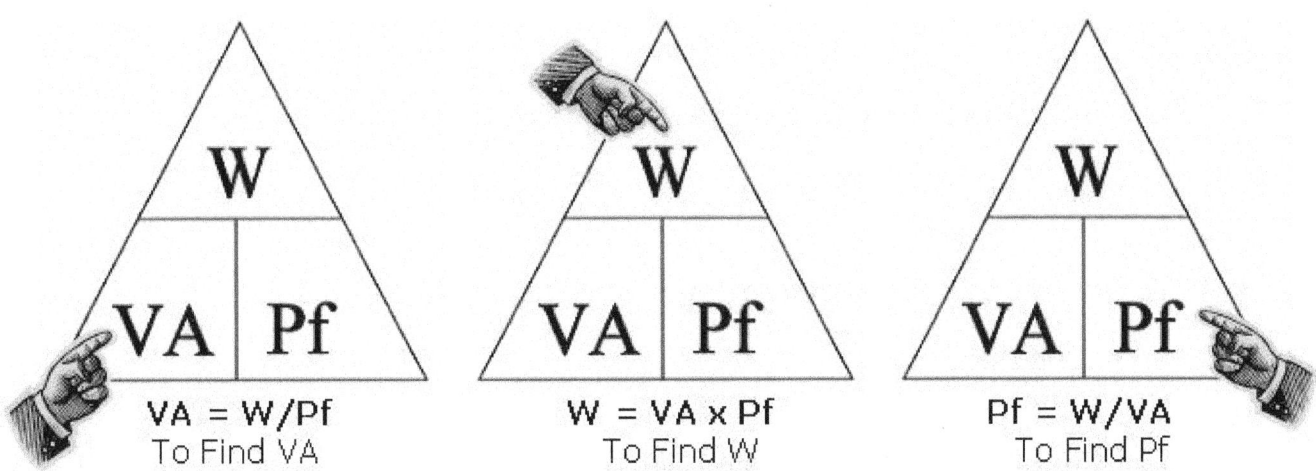

Copyright© 2016

VOLTAGE DROP FORMULAS

Formula Definitions:

VD = Volts dropped from a circuit.

2 = Multiplying factor for single-phase circuits. The 2 represents the conductor length in a single-phase circuit.

1.732 = Multiplying factor for three-phase circuits. The square root of 3 represents the conductor length in a three-phase circuit.

The only difference between the single-phase and three-phase **formulas is that "1.732" has replaced "2"**.

K = Approximate resistivity of the conductor per mil foot. A mil foot is a wire 1 foot long and one mil in diameter. The approximate K value for copper wire is **12.9** ohms and for aluminum wire is **21.2** ohms per mil foot.

I = Current or amperage draw of the load.

D = The distance from the source voltage to the load.

CM = Circular mil area of the conductor. (Chapter 9, Table 8)

*NOTE – When determining wire size, distance or current, VD is the actual volts that can be dropped from the circuit. The recommended percentage for a branch-circuit is 3%. Example: 3% of 120 volts is 3.6 volts. DO NOT enter 3% in the VD position.

To find voltage drop in a single-phase circuit.

$$VD = \frac{2 \times K \times I \times D}{CM}$$

To find wire size in a single-phase circuit.

$$CM = \frac{2 \times K \times I \times D}{VD}$$

To find distance in a single-phase circuit.

$$D = \frac{CM \times VD}{2 \times K \times I}$$

To find MAXIMUM current in amperes in a single-phase circuit.

$$I = \frac{CM \times VD}{2 \times K \times D}$$

Commonly used NEC® Tables and Articles:

Tbl. 110.26(A)(1)	Working Spaces About Electrical Equipment of 600 Volts or Less
Tbl. 110.28	Enclosure Selection
210.8	GFCI Protection
210.12	AFCI Protection
Tbl. 210.21(B)(3)	Receptacle Ratings
Tbl. 210.24	Branch-Circuit Requirements
Tbl. 220.12	General Lighting Loads by Occupancy
Tbl. 220.42	Lighting Load Demand Factors
Tbl. 220.55	Demand Factors for Household Cooking Appliances
Tbl. 220.56	Demand Factors for Commercial Kitchen Equipment
Tbl. 220.84	Optional Calculation-Demand Factors for Multi-Family Dwellings
240.6(A)	Standard Ampere Ratings of Overcurrent Protection Devices
Tbl. 250.66	Grounding Electrode Conductor
Tbl. 250.122	Equipment Grounding Conductors
Tbl. 300.5	Burial Depth of Conductors and Cables
Tbl. 310.15(B)(2)(a)	Ambient Temperature Correction Factors for Conductors
Tbl. 310.15(B)(3)(a)	Adjustment Factors for More Than 3 Wires in Raceway
Tbl. 310.15(B)(2)(c)	Temperature Adjustment for Rooftop Conductors and Conduits
Tbl. 310.15(B)(7)	Dwelling Service & Feeder Conductor Sizing
Tbl. 310.15(B)(16)	Allowable Ampacities of Conductors in Raceways
Tbl. 310.15(B)(17)	Allowable Ampacities of Single Conductors in Free Air
Tbl. 310.104(A)	Conductor Applications and Insulations
430.32	Overload Sizing for Motors
Tbl. 430.52	Motor Overcurrent Protection
Tbl. 430.248	Single-Phase Motors Full-Load Current Ratings
Tbl. 430.250	Three-Phase Motors Full-Load Current Ratings
Tbl. 450.3(A)	Overcurrent Protection for Transformers Over 600 Volts
Tbl. 450.4(A)	Overcurrent Protection for Transformers of 600 Volts or Less
Chpt. 9, Tbl. 4	Dimensions and Percent Area of Conduit and Tubing
Chpt. 9, Tbl. 5	Dimensions of Insulated Conductors
Chpt. 9, Tbl. 8	Conductor Properties
Annex C	Conduit and Tubing Fill for Conductors of the Same Size
Annex D	Calculation Examples

ELECTRICIANS PRACTICE EXAMS
MAINTENANCE ELECTRICIAN
EXAM #1

The following questions are based on the 2011 edition of the National Electrical Code® and are typical of questions encountered on most Maintenance Electricians' Licensing Exams. Select the best answer from the choices given and review your answers with the answer key included in this book.

ALLOTTED TIME: 75 minutes

1. Which of the following listed does the NEC® define as utilization equipment?

A. water heater
B. thermal overload device
C. motor controller
D. molded circuit breaker

2. Concealed is defined as being _____ .

A. not readily visible
B. made inacessible by the structure or finish of the building
C. surrounded by walls
D. attached to the surface

3. Electrical wiring installed under canopies or roofed open porches is considered to be installed in a _____ location.

A. damp
B. wet
C. dry
D. moist

4. Ohm's Law is a relationship between _____ .

A. voltage, current and power
B. voltage, current and resistance
C. voltage, current and wattage
D. voltage, current and power factor

5. Which of the following is a unit of electrical power?

A. watt
B. voltage
C. resistance
D. conductance

6. When checking for continuity between a circuit breaker and the neutral bar of a panelboard when using a continuity tester, positive continuity is indicated. The reason may be _____.

   I. a conductor grounded
   a luminaire or an appliance may be turned on

A. I only
B. II only
C. either I or II
D. neither I nor II

7. When installing electrical metallic tubing, (EMT) there shall be no more than _____ 90 degree bends in the tubing between boxes and/or pull points.

A. three
B. four
C. five
D. six

8. The full-load running current of a 3 hp, 208-volt, single-phase, ac motor used in a continuous duty application is _____.

A. 10.6 amperes
B. 19.6 amperes
C. 13.2 amperes
D. 18.7 amperes

9. The NEC® mandates specific branch-circuits, receptacle outlets and utilization equipment to be provided with a ground-fault circuit interrupter (GFCI); this device is intended _____ .

A. to prevent overloading the conductors
B. to prevent overloading the circuit breakers
C. for the protection of equipment from overloads
D. for the protection of personnel

Unused openings in metal boxes, cabinets, and other such enclosures shall be _____.

A. left open
B. effectively closed
C. not required to be closed, if on the bottom of the enclosure
D. not required to be closed if the enclosure is in a dry area

11. What is the MINIMUM height required for the working space in front of a 120/240 volt, single-phase, 400 ampere rated disconnect switch located in a commercial occupancy?

A. 6 feet
B. 6 feet, 3 inches
C. 6 feet, 6 inches
D. 8 feet

12. What is the largest size insulated solid conductor permitted by the NEC® to be pulled in an existing raceway?

A. 4 AWG
B. 6 AWG
C. 8 AWG
D. 10 AWG

13. If the voltage drop of a branch circuit is too great, which of the following, if any, may be the result?

   I. unsatisfactory illumination of luminaires
   overheating of a motor or unsatisfactory motor speed

A. I only
B. II only
C. both I and II
D. neither I nor II

14. Which one of the following listed circuit breakers is NOT a standard ampere rating?

A. 110 amperes
B. 90 amperes
C. 75 amperes
D. 225 amperes

15. A 4 in. x 1½ in. metal octagon box may contain a MAXIMUM of _____ size 14 AWG conductors.

A. six
B. seven
C. nine
D. ten

16. In general, electrical nonmetallic tubing (ENT) shall be securely fastened at intervals NOT exceeding _____.

A. 10 feet
B. 6 feet
C. 4 feet
D. 3 feet

17. In general, when a 20-ampere branch circuit serves a single receptacle outlet, the rating of the receptacle must NOT be less than _____.

A. 10 amperes
B. 15 amperes
C. 16 amperes
D. 20 amperes

18. The branch-circuit conductors supplying a 7½ hp, 240-volt, single-phase, induction type, ac motor used in a continuous duty application, shall have a MINIMUM ampacity of _____.

A. 60 amperes
B. 40 amperes
C. 50 amperes
D. 75 amperes

19. Where the copper conductors supplying the previous referenced motor have a temperature rating of 75 degrees C, determine the MINIMUM size as required by the NEC®.

A. 8 AWG
B. 6 AWG
C. 10 AWG
D. 4 AWG

20. A type of fuse NOT permitted for new installations and shall be used only for replacements in existing installations is a _____ fuse.

A. Class K
B. Class H renewable cartridge
C. Class CC
D. Time delay

A 240-volt, single-phase 10 kW commercial dishwasher will have a full-load current rating of _____.

A. 21 amperes
B. 24 amperes
C. 42 amperes
D. 30 amperes

22. The ampacity of a conductor is defined by the NEC® to be the maximum current, in amperes, a conductor can carry continuously under the conditions of use without exceeding _____ .

A. it's temperature rating
B. the allowable voltage drop limitations
C. it's melting point
D. it's rated voltage

23. A conductor with THHN marked on the insulation has a temperature rating of _____ .

A. 90 degrees F
B. 90 degrees C
C. 75 degrees F
D. 75 degrees C

24. A 120 volt, single-phase, branch circuit is to supply fifteen (15), 150 watt incandescent luminaires. Determine the current in this branch circuit.

A. 36.50 amperes
B. 18.75 amperes
C. 9.37 amperes
D. 14.1 amperes

25. In general, the MAXIMUM height to the center of the operating handle of a disconnect switch when it is in the ON position, must NOT exceed _____ above the floor or working platform.

A. 5 feet, 6 inches
B. 6 feet
C. 6 feet, 6 inches
D. 6 feet, 7 inches

END OF EXAM #1

ELECTRICIANS PRACTICE EXAMS
MAINTENANCE ELECTRICIAN
EXAM #2

The following questions are based on the 2011 edition of the National Electrical Code® and are typical of questions encountered on most Maintenance Electricians' Licensing Exams. Select the best answer from the choices given and review your answers with the answer key included in this book.

ALLOTTED TIME: 75 minutes

1. The MAXIMUM current load, in amperes, on a size 6 AWG THHN copper conductor is permitted to be _____ where connected to a fusible disconnect switch with terminals rated for 75 degrees C.

A. 75 amperes
B. 65 amperes
C. 60 amperes
D. 55 amperes

2. Under normal conditions, the grounding conductor will:

A. improve current flow.
B. not carry current.
C. carry current.
D. reduce circuit resistance.

3. Compliance with the provisions of the NEC® will result in an electrical installation that is essentially _____.

A. free from hazard
B. a good electrical system
C. an efficient system
D. all of these

4. The ratio of the maximum demand of an electrical system to the connected load of the system is known as the _____ of the system.

A. full-load current
B. full-load amperes
C. demand factor
D. ratio factor

5. A megger is used to measure _____.

A. reactance
B. insulation resistance
C. specific gravity
D. current

6. An ac motor that has nine (9) leads coming out of it is a _____.

A. two-phase motor
B. two speed motor
C. dual voltage motor
D. multi-speed motor

7. On a 4-wire, delta-connected system, the conductor having the higher voltage to ground, (high-leg) shall be identified as _____ in color, if the grounded conductor is also present to supply lighting or similar loads.

A. white
B. red
C. green
D. orange

8. When an electrical trade size 3/4 in. electrical metallic tubing (EMT) is more than 24 inches in length, the EMT is permitted to contain NO more than _____ size 10 AWG conductors with THWN insulation.

A. 14
B. 10
C. 8
D. 6

9. When a conduit or tubing having a length of more than 24 inches contains four (4) current-carrying conductors, an adjustment factor of _____ must be applied to the conductor ampacity values given in Table 310.15(B)(16) of the NEC®.

A. 90 percent
B. 80 percent
C. 75 percent
D. 70 percent

The reason the NEC® requires all grounded and ungrounded conductors of a common circuit to be grouped together in the same metal raceway is to reduce _____.

A. expense
B. inductive heat
C. voltage drop
D. resistance

11. In general, electrical metallic tubing (EMT) shall be securely fastened within _____ of each junction box, panelboard or other conduit termination.

A. 3 feet
B. 6 feet
C. 8 feet
D. 10 feet

For the purpose of determining the allowable ampacity of a copper conductor with THWN insulation installed in a raceway located in an area where the ambient temperature reaches 100 degrees F, a temperature correction factor of _____ must be applied to the ampacity values given in Table 310.15(B)(16) of the NEC®.

A. 0.94
B. 0.88
C. 0.82
D. 0.75

13. For motors used in a continuous-duty application, the motor nameplate current rating is used to determine the size of the _____ required for the motor.

A. disconnecting means
B. branch-circuit conductors
C. motor overload protection
D. short-circuit protection

14. In general, branch circuits conductors supplying a continuous-duty, ac motor shall have an ampacity of NOT less than _____ of the full-load current rating of the motor.

A. 125 percent
B. 100 percent
C. 150 percent
D. 115 percent

15. AC voltages may be increased or decreased by use of a/an _____.

A. rectifier
B. motor
C. transformer
D. overload device

16. When circuit breakers are used to switch 120-volt and 277-volt fluorescent lighting circuits, the circuit breakers shall be listed and marked _____ .

   I. SWD
   HID

A. I only
B. II only
C. either I or II
D. neither I nor II

17. A 15 kW, 208-volt, single-phase heat pump has a full-load current rating of _____ .

A. 72 amperes
B. 46 amperes
C. 66 amperes
D. 33 amperes

18. Where an insulated black conductor is identified by three (3) continuous white stripes along its entire length, it is considered a/an _____.

A. grounded conductor
B. ungrounded conductor
C. equipment grounding conductor
D. phase of a delta-connected system

19. Where a 9 kW, 208-volt, 3-phase electric steamer is to be installed in a commercial establishment; the steamer will draw _____ of current.

A. 43 amperes
B. 4.3 amperes
C. 25 amperes
D. 75 amperes

20. What is the approximate MAXIMUM distance a single-phase, 240-volt, 42 ampere load can be located from a panelboard, where given the following related information?

copper conductors - K = 12.9
size 8 AWG THWN/THHN conductors are used
Limit voltage drop to 3 percent

A. 50 feet
B. 110 feet
C. 160 feet
D. 195 feet

21. The NEC® permits electrical trade size 3/8 in. flexible metal conduit (FMC) to be used for tap conductors to luminaires, provided the length of the flex does NOT exceed _____ .

A. four feet
B. six feet
C. eight feet
D. ten feet

22. The MINIMUM required width of the working space in front of panelboards, switchboards, disconnects and motor controllers, shall be the width of the equipment or _____, whichever is greater.

A. 2 feet
B. 3 feet
C. 4 feet
D. 30 inches

23. In general, branch circuit conductors serving continuous loads, such as fluorescent lighting in an office building, school classroom, or retail shopping mall, shall have an ampacity of NOT less than _____ of the load.

A. 125 percent
B. 115 percent
C. 150 percent
D. 80 percent

24. Where two (2) or more general-purpose receptacle outlets are connected to a branch circuit having a rating of 20-amperes, the receptacles are required to have an ampere rating of _____.

   I. 15 amperes
   20 amperes

A. I only
B. II only
C. either I or II
D. neither I nor II

25. In general, the overcurrent protection for size 12 AWG copper conductors, regardless of the insulation type shall NOT exceed _____ after any correction factors for ambient temperature and number of conductors have been applied.

A. 15 amperes
B. 20 amperes
C. 25 amperes
D. 30 amperes

END OF EXAM #2

ELECTRICIANS PRACTICE EXAMS
RESIDENTIAL ELECTRICIAN
EXAM #3

The following questions are based on the 2011 edition of the National Electrical Code® and are typical of questions encountered on most Residential Electricians' Licensing Exams. Select the best answer from the choices given and review your answers with the answer key included in this book.

ALLOTED TIME: 75 minutes

1. In a dwelling unit that has more than one bathroom, the receptacle outlets shall be supplied by at LEAST _____ .

A. one 15-ampere branch circuit which supplies no other outlets
B. one 20-ampere branch circuit which supplies no other outlets
C. one 15-ampere branch circuit which is also permitted to serve bathroom lighting
D. one 20-ampere branch circuit which is also permitted to serve bathroom lighting

2. In general, all 120-volt, single-phase, 15- and 20-ampere branch circuits supplying outlets installed in dwelling units shall be protected by a listed arc-fault circuit interrupter. An exception to this rule is outlets installed in _____ .

A. hallways
B. dining rooms
C. kitchens
D. living rooms

3. All 125-volt, single-phase receptacles not exceeding 30 amperes located at LEAST within _____ of the inside wall of a hydromassage tub shall be protected by a GFCI.

A. 3 feet
B. 5 feet
C. 6 feet
D. 10 feet

4. Surface mounted incandescent luminaires are permitted to be installed above the door, or on the ceiling of a clothes closet, provided there is a MINIMUM clearance of _____ between the luminaire and the nearest shelf.

A. 6 inches
B. 8 inches
C. 12 inches
D. 18 inches

5. A receptacle installed for a washing machine in the laundry room of a dwelling unit must be installed within at LEAST _____ of the intended location of the appliance.

A. 6 feet
B. 4 feet
C. 3 feet
D. 10 feet

6. Which of the following conductors need overcurrent protection on a residential electric service?

A. grounding conductor
B. bonding conductor
C. identified conductors
D. ungrounded conductors

7. Where a 40 gallon electric water heater to be installed has a nameplate rating of 4,500 watts @ 240 volts, single-phase, what is the MAXIMUM standard size overcurrent protection device the NEC® allows to protect this water heater?

A. 20 amperes
B. 25 amperes
C. 30 amperes
D. 45 amperes

8. Tap conductors for recessed luminaires shall be in a suitable raceway of at LEAST _____ in length.

A. 18 inches
B. 2 feet
C. 4 feet
D. 6 feet

9. In general, the power supply cord to a mobile home shall have a MAXIMUM rating of _____.

A. 50 amperes
B. 60 amperes
C. 100 amperes
D. 150 amperes

10. When calculating the demand load for a one-family dwelling, what total MINIMUM volt-amperes (VA) must be included in the calculation for the small-appliance and laundry circuit loads?

A. 6,000 VA
B. 4,500 VA
C. 3,000 VA
D. 1,500 VA

11. When the heating, air-conditioning or refrigeration equipment is installed on the roof of an apartment building, a 15- or 20-ampere, 125-volt, rated receptacle _____ .

A. is not required by the NEC®
B. may be connected to the line side of the equipment disconnecting means, if the outlet is GFCI protected
C. shall be located on the same level and within 25 feet of the heating, air-conditioning, or refrigeration equipment
D. shall be installed on the roof where the equipment is located and not more than 75 feet from each unit

12. The MINIMUM number of 120-volt, 15-ampere, general lighting branch circuits required for a dwelling with 70 feet by 30 feet of livable space is _____.

A. two
B. three
C. four
D. five

13. All 15- and 20-ampere, 125-volt, single-phase receptacles installed in a residential garage must be _____.

A. provided with AFCI protection
B. provided with GFCI protection
C. provided with a metal faceplate
D. a single receptacle

14. In general, service conductors installed as open conductors shall have a clearance of NOT less than _____ from windows that are designed to be opened, porches, doors or balconies.

A. 6 feet
B. 8 feet
C. 5 feet
D. 3 feet

15. A 120-volt branch circuit is to have only six (6) 100 watt incandescent lighting fixtures connected. What will be the total measured current in the home run supplying this load?

A. 30 amperes
B. 20 amperes
C. 5 amperes
D. 12 amperes

16. At the electrical service provided for a residence, the service-drop conductors shall have a MINIMUM clearance from final grade of _____ .

A. 8 feet
B. 10 feet
C. 12 feet
D. 15 feet

17. Electrical outlet boxes installed in walls and ceilings shall be _____ .

A. inacessible
B. readily accessible
C. accessible
D. metal

18. In a dwelling unit bedroom, any wall space that is at LEAST _____ or more in width must be provided with a general-use receptacle outlet.

A. 2 feet
B. 4 feet
C. 6 feet
D. 10 feet

19. Metallic surface type cabinets for electrical equipment in damp or wet locations, shall be mounted so there is at LEAST _____ air space between the cabinet and the wall or other supporting surface.

A. 1/8 inch
B. 1/4 inch
C. 3/8 inch
D. 1/2 inch

20. In dwelling units, hallways of _____ or more in length shall have at least one receptacle outlet.

A. 10 feet
B. 20 feet
C. 25 feet
D. 30 feet

21. Receptacles in a kitchen of a residence that are to serve countertop surfaces, shall be installed that no point along the wall line is more than _____ , measured horizontally from a receptacle outlet in that space.

A. 24 inches
B. 18 inches
C. 36 inches
D. 48 inches

22. Where you are to install a 20-ampere, 120-volt, GFCI protected, direct-buried branch circuit, using Type UF cable, that serves landscape lighting for a residence, what is the MINIMUM ground cover required for the cable?

A. 6 inches
B. 12 inches
C. 18 inches
D. 24 inches

23. Where NM cable is run at angles with joists in unfinished basements, it shall be permissible to secure cables NOT smaller than _____ , directly to the lower edges of the joists.

A. 10/2 AWG
B. 8/2 AWG
C. 6/2 AWG
D. 6/3 AWG

24. At the time of installation, grounded (neutral) conductors larger than size 6 AWG may be identified at its terminations by _____ colored phase tape.

A. white
B. orange
C. red
D. blue

25. Three-way and four-way switches shall be so wired that all switching is done:

A. only in the grounded circuit conductor.
B. only in the ungrounded circuit conductor.
C. either in the grounded or ungrounded circuit conductor.
D. only in the white circuit conductor.

END OF EXAM #3

ELECTRICIANS PRACTICE EXAMS
RESIDENTIAL ELECTRICIAN
EXAM #4

The following questions are based on the 2011 edition of the National Electrical Code® and are typical of questions encountered on most Residential Electricians' Licensing Exams. Select the best answer from the choices given and review your answers with the answer key included in this book.

ALLOTTED TIME: 75 minutes

1. In general, for dwelling units, receptacle outlets required for the kitchen countertops, must be located above, but NOT more than _____ above the countertop.

A. 12 inches
B. 18 inches
C. 20 inches
D. 24 inches

2. For dwelling units, panelboards are permitted to be located in all the areas listed EXCEPT _____ .

A. hallways
B. garages
C. kitchens
D. bathrooms

3. Overhead spans of open conductors of not over 300 volts to ground shall have a clearance of NOT less than _____ over residential driveways.

A. 10 feet
B. 12 feet
C. 15 feet
D. 18 feet

4. What is the MINIMUM number of 120-volt, 15-ampere, general lighting branch circuits required for a dwelling unit having a connected lighting load of 9,600 VA?

A. three
B. four
C. five
D. six

5. When a 125-volt receptacle outlet is installed on a kitchen island countertop in a residence and it is 8 feet from the kitchen sink, which of the following statements, if any, is correct?

A. GFCI protection is not required because the receptacle is not within 6 feet of the sink.
B. GFCI protection is required for all countertop kitchen receptacles.
C. GFCI protection is not required on receptacles installed on kitchen islands.
D. None of the above.

6. A two (2) gang device box is to contain two (2) size 12/2 AWG w/ground NM cables connected to a duplex receptacle and two (2) size 14/2 AWG w/ground NM cables connected to a single-pole switch. The two (2) gang box will also contain four (4) cable clamps. What MINIMUM volume, in cubic inches, is required of the box?

A. 28 cubic inches
B. 30 cubic inches
C. 34 cubic inches
D. 36 cubic inches

7. A GFCI protected receptacle that provides power to a swimming pool recirculating pump motor, shall be permitted NOT less than _____ from the inside wall of a permanently installed swimming pool.

A. 10 feet
B. 5 feet
C. 6 feet
D. 12 feet

8. Panelboards containing circuit breakers are NOT permitted to be located _____ .

   I. within 6 feet of a water heater
   over steps of stairways

A. I only
B. II only
C. both I and II
D. neither I nor II

9. Any one cord-and-plug-connected utilization equipment connected to a 20-ampere branch circuit shall have a MAXIMUM rating of _____.

A. 10 amperes
B. 16 amperes
C. 20 amperes
D. 25 amperes

10. In dwelling units, which of the following outlet(s) are permitted to be connected to the branch-circuit provided to supply the laundry receptacle outlet(s)?

A. Luminaires in the laundry room.
B. Receptacle outlets in the bathroom.
C. One receptacle outlet only in the hallway.
D. None of these.

11. For a one-family dwelling, the service disconnecting means shall have a rating of NOT less than _____ when supplied with a 120/240 volt, 3-wire, single-phase, service.

A. 30 amperes
B. 60 amperes
C. 100 amperes
D. 200 amperes

12. A one-family dwelling is to have three (3) wall-mounted ovens rated 6, 8, and 3.5 kW, a cooktop rated 6 kW and a broiler rated 3.5 kW. The MINIMUM feeder demand on the ungrounded conductors is _____ when applying the general method of calculation for dwellings.

A. 12.2 kW
B. 18.6 kW
C. 27.3 kW
D. 30.1 kW

13. The service equipment for a mobile home shall be rated NOT less than _____ , 120/240 volts, single-phase.

A. 50 amperes
B. 60 amperes
C. 100 amperes
D. 150 amperes

14. Outside open conductors of not over 600 volts shall have a clearance of NOT less than _____ from signs, chimneys, and TV antennas.

A. 8 feet
B. 6 feet
C. 4 feet
D. 3 feet

15. When the ungrounded service-entrance conductors for a residence are size 3/0 AWG copper conductors, a copper grounding electrode conductor attached to the concrete-encased steel reinforcing bars used as the grounding electrode shall be NOT smaller than size _____ .

A. 2 AWG
B. 4 AWG
C. 6 AWG
D. 8 AWG

16. What is the MAXIMUM time period allowed for temporary outdoor Christmas decoration lighting for residences?

A. 30 days
B. 60 days
C. 90 days
four months

17. A luminaire stud in an outlet box is considered the equivalent of how many conductors?

A. none
B. one
C. two
D. three

18. A branch circuit supplying more than one electric baseboard heater in a residential occupancy shall be rated a MAXIMUM of _____ .

A. 15 amperes
B. 20 amperes
C. 30 amperes
D. 50 amperes

19. In general, when installing electrical metallic tubing (EMT), the run of tubing is required to be securely fastened at LEAST every _____ .

A. 6 feet
B. 10 feet
C. 15 feet
D. 20 feet

20. The service disconnecting means for each residential service shall consist of NOT more than _____ switch(es) or set(s) of circuit breakers.

A. one
B. two
C. four
D. six

21. The ampacity of UF cable shall be that of _____ conductors.

A. 60 deg. C
B. 75 deg. C
C. 85 deg. C
D. 90 deg. C

22. The front edge of a switch box installed in a wall constructed of wood shall be _____ from the surface of the wall.

A. flush with or projected out
B. set back a maximum of 1/4 in.
C. set back a maximum of 1/2 in.
D. set back a maximum of 3/8 in.

23. For dwelling units, where receptacle outlets are installed within at LEAST _____ of the outside edge of a sink in a laundry room, GFCI protection must be provided.

A. 5 feet
B. 6 feet
C. 8 feet
D. 10 feet

24. For dwelling units, a branch circuit supplying _____ receptacle outlets is permitted to also supply receptacles in an attached garage.

A. outdoor
B. bathroom
C. laundry room
D. kitchen small appliance

25. A metal underground water pipe may serve as a grounding electrode if it is in direct contact with the earth for at LEAST _____ or more.

A. 6 feet
B. 8 feet
C. 10 feet
D. 12 feet

END OF EXAM #4

ELECTRICIANS PRACTICE EXAMS
RESIDENTIAL ELECTRICIAN
EXAM #5

The following questions are based on the 2011 edition of the National Electrical Code® and are typical of questions encountered on most Residential Electricians' Licensing Exams. Select the best answer from the choices given and review your answers with the answer key included in this book.

ALLOTTED TIME: 75 minutes

1. What is the MAXIMUM allowable cord length for a cord-and-plug-connected dishwasher installed under a counter in a dwelling unit?

A. 1½ feet
B. 2 feet
C. 3 feet
D. 4 feet

2. What is the MINIMUM size copper SE cable with type THHW insulation that may be used as ungrounded service-entrance conductors for a 150 ampere, 120/240 volt, single-phase residential service?

A. 1/0 AWG
B. 1 AWG
C. 2 AWG
D. 3 AWG

3. For outlet boxes designed to support ceiling-suspended (paddle) fans that weigh MORE than _____ , the required marking shall include the maximum weight to be supported.

A. 20 pounds
B. 30 pounds
C. 35 pounds
D. 70 pounds

4. A connection to a driven or buried grounding electrode shall _____ .

A. be accessible
B. not be required to be accessible
C. not permitted to be buried
D. be visible

5. In general, the MINIMUM size overhead service-drop conductors permitted for a dwelling unit is _____ .

A. 8 AWG copper or 6 AWG aluminum
B. 6 AWG copper or 4 AWG aluminum
C. 4 AWG copper or 1 AWG aluminum
D. 2 AWG copper or 3 AWG aluminum

6. The MAXIMUM number of size 10 AWG conductors permitted in a 4 in. x 1¼ in. octagon metal junction box is _____.

A. two
B. four
C. five
D. six

7. Determine the MINIMUM number of 15-ampere, 120-volt, general lighting branch-circuits required for a dwelling with 2,600 square feet of habitable space.

A. three
B. four
C. five
D. six

8. When calculating the total load on a dwelling, what is the MINIMUM volt-amps (VA) that must be included for the general-use receptacle outlets?

A. none
B. one VA
C. two VA
D. three VA

9. A cord-and-attachment-plug connected room air-conditioner shall NOT exceed _____ of the rating of the branch-circuit where lighting outlets or general-use receptacles are also supplied.

A. 80 percent
B. 75 percent
C. 60 percent
D. 50 percent

10. It shall be permissible to apply a demand factor of _____ to the nameplate-rating load of four (4) or more fastened in place water heaters located in a multifamily dwelling unit, where applying the standard method of calculation for dwellings.

A. 50 percent
B. 75 percent
C. 80 percent
D. 60 percent

11. In dwelling units, at least one receptacle outlet shall be installed in bathrooms; the outlet shall be within at LEAST _____ of the outside edge of each basin.

A. 12 inches
B. 18 inches
C. 24 inches
D. 36 inches

12. When installing Type NM cable through bored holes in wooden studs, the holes shall be bored so that the edge of the hole is NOT less than _____ from the edge, or the cable shall be protected by a steel plate at least 1/16 inch thick.

A. 3/4 inch
B. 1 inch
C. 1¼ inches
D. 1½ inches

13. A 240-volt, single-phase, 30-ampere rated electric clothes dryer has a volt-amp (VA) rating of _____ .

A. 5,000 VA
B. 7,200 VA
C. 8,000 VA
D. 15,400 VA

14. Type XHHW insulated conductors may be used in _____ .

A. dry locations only
B. wet locations only
C. dry or damp locations only
D. dry, damp, or wet locations

15. In kitchens of dwelling units, a receptacle outlet shall be installed at each usable wall countertop space that is at LEAST _____ or wider.

A. 10 inches
B. 12 inches
C. 18 inches
D. 24 inches

16. When doing residential service and feeder calculations, clothes dryers are to be calculated at a MINIMUM of _____ watts (VA), or the nameplate rating, whichever is larger.

A. 3,000
B. 4,500
C. 5,000
D. 6,000

17. The rating of any single cord-and-plug-connected appliance connected to a 30-ampere rated branch circuit shall NOT exceed _____ .

A. 30 amperes
B. 27 amperes
C. 24 amperes
D. 16 amperes

18. Ground-fault circuit interrupter protection MUST be provided in residential kitchens for receptacles that _____.

A. serve the countertop surface
B. also serve the dining room
C. are on the same circuit as the outdoor receptacles
D. are beneath the countertop

19. A branch circuit supplying a 5 kW wall-mounted oven and a 7 kW counter-mounted cooktop in a residence, will have a demand factor of _____ on the ungrounded service-entrance and feeder conductors where applying the standard method of calculation for dwelling units.

A. 12.0 kW
B. 9.5 kW
C. 8.0 kW
D. 7.8 kW

20. The MINIMUM size copper equipment grounding conductor required to bond equipment supplied by a 40-ampere branch circuit is _____ .

A. 10 AWG
B. 8 AWG
C. 12 AWG
D. 14 AWG

21. What is the MAXIMUM allowable voltage between conductors on a branch circuit supplying luminaires in a residence?

A. 120 volts
B. 150 volts
C. 240 volts
D. 250 volts

22. The ampacity of the branch-circuit conductors to a residential central heating electric furnace shall NOT be less than _____ of the furnace load.

A. 80 percent
B. 100 percent
C. 115 percent
D. 125 percent

Copyright© 2016

23. Rod and pipe grounding electrodes shall be permitted to be buried in a trench _____ .

A. under all circumstances
B. under no circumstances
C. that has a depth of 2 feet
D. when rock bottom is encountered

24. The NEC® requires recessed portions of lighting fixture enclosures that are not identified for contact with insulation, to be spaced from combustible material a MINIMUM of _____ .

A. 3/8 in.
B. 1/2 in.
C. 3/4 in.
D. 1 in.

25. Type NM cable is NOT permitted for use _____.

A. in wet locations
B. in Type V construction
C. for exposed work
D. in any of the above listed installations

END OF EXAM #5

ELECTRICIANS PRACTICE EXAMS
RESIDENTIAL ELECTRICIAN
EXAM #6

The following questions are based on the 2011 edition of the National Electrical Code® and are typical of questions encountered on most Residential Electricians' Licensing Exams. Select the best answer from the choices given and review your answers with the answer key included in this book.

ALLOTTED TIME: 75 minutes

1. A point on a wiring system at which current is taken to supply utilization equipment is known as a/an _____.

A. outlet
B. wall switch
C. load center
D. panelboard

2. The point of attachment of a service-drop to a residence where the voltage is 120-volts to ground is a MINIMUM of _____ above final grade level.

A. 8 feet
B. 10 feet
C. 12 feet
D. 15 feet

3. The required MINIMUM working space, in feet, in front of 120/240 volt, single-phase service equipment when grounded parts are opposite the service is _____ .

A. 2 feet
B. 2½ feet
C. 3 feet
D. 4 feet

4. When installing an overhead service using a rigid metal conduit (RMC) service mast for the support of service-drop conductors, the mast shall be of adequate strength or be _____ .

A. a minimum of 2 inches in diameter
B. a minimum of 3 inches in diameter
C. supported by braces or guys
D. less than 4 feet in length

5. The MINIMUM distance from wall switches to the inside walls of an indoor installed spa or hot tub shall be _____ .

A. 5 feet
B. 10 feet
C. 15 feet
D. 18 feet

6. All 15- and 20-ampere, single-phase, 125-volt receptacles located at LEAST within _____ of the inside walls of a permanently installed swimming pool shall be protected by a GFCI.

A. 10 feet
B. 15 feet
C. 20 feet
D. 25 feet

7. A luminaire shall be supported independently of the outlet box where it weighs MORE than _____ unless the outlet box is listed for the weight to be supported.

A. 6 pounds
B. 25 pounds
C. 35 pounds
D. 50 pounds

8. As per the NEC®, the full-load current rating of a 3/4 hp, 120-volt, single-phase, ac motor is _____.

A. 9.8 amperes
B. 13.8 amperes
C. 7.9 amperes
D. 16.0 amperes

Copyright© 2016

9. A ground rod is required to be driven a MINIMUM of _____ into the soil.

A. 4 feet
B. 6 feet
C. 8 feet
D. 10 feet

10. Receptacle outlets are permitted to be installed directly over a bathtub or shower stall _____.

A. if the outlet has a weatherproof cover
B. if the outlet is GFCI protected
C. if the outlet has a weatherproof cover and is GFCI protected
D. never

11. What is the MAXIMUM allowable ampacity of size 14/2 AWG type SJT cord?

A. 15 amperes
B. 13 amperes
C. 20 amperes
D. 18 amperes

12. Where a listed packaged spa or hot tub is installed outdoors, the unit is permitted to be cord-and-plug connected, provided the cord is NOT longer than _____ and protected by a GFCI.

A. 6 feet
B. 10 feet
C. 15 feet
D. 20 feet

13. The ampacity of branch-circuit conductors and the rating or setting of overcurrent protective devices supplying fixed outdoor electric deicing equipment shall NOT be less than _____ of the full-load current of the equipment.

A. 100 percent
B. 125 percent
C. 80 percent
D. 150 percent

14. What is the MINIMUM burial depth of intermediate metal conduit, (IMC) containing 100 ampere rated, 240-volt, single-phase, conductors where located under a residential gravel driveway?

A. 12 inches
B. 18 inches
C. 24 inches
D. 30 inches

15. Disregarding exceptions, where residential lighting outlets are installed in interior stairways, there shall be a wall switch provided _____ .

A. near the stairs
B. every seven (7) steps
C. at the top and bottom of the stairs if there are more than six (6) steps
D. at any convenient location

16. The MAXIMUM distance between supports for trade size 3/4 in. Schedule 40 PVC conduit is _____ .

A. 8 feet
B. 6 feet
C. 4 feet
D. 3 feet

17. A metal box or terminal fitting having separately bushed holes for each conductor, shall be used whenever change is made from conduit to _____ .

A. knob-and-tube wiring
B. nonmetallic sheathed cable (NM)
C. type AC cable
D. type MC cable

18. When sizing the overcurrent protection for a single non-motor operated appliance, which of the following need NOT to be taken into consideration?

A. The length of time the appliance operates.
B. The voltage rating of the appliance.
C. The full-load current marked on the appliance.
D. Where the overcurrent protection selected is not a standard size.

Copyright© 2016

19. Concealed knob-and-tube wiring shall be permitted to be used only for _____ , unless special permission is granted by the local inspector.

A. dwellings
B. extensions of existing installations
C. accessible installations
D. temporary wiring

20. In dwelling units, receptacle outlets installed within six (6) feet of the outside edge of a sink in a laundry room shall _____ .

A. have a weatherproof cover
B. have AFCI protection
C. be a single receptacle
D. be provided with GFCI protection

21. When bending Type NM cable, the tightest bend permitted by the NEC®, has a radius of _____ times the diameter of the cable.

A. five
B. six
C. seven
D. eight

22. For the purpose of determining box fill, size 12 AWG THWN copper conductors are to be calculated at _____ per conductor.

A. 1.75 cubic inches
B. 2.00 cubic inches
C. 2.25 cubic inches
D. 2.50 square inches

23. What is the MAXIMUM distance allowed between supports, such as staples, when installing nonmetallic sheathed cable (NM)?

A. 3 feet
B. 4½ feet
C. 6 feet
D. 10 feet

24. Without exceptions being considered, the MINIMUM size service-lateral conductors allowed by the NEC® is _____.

A. 8 AWG copper
B. 6 AWG copper
C. 4 AWG aluminum
D. 2 AWG aluminum

25. How many size 12/2 AWG with ground, Type NM cables are permitted to be installed in an outlet box with a volume of 18 cubic inches where a duplex receptacle is housed in the box?

A. one
B. two
C. three
D. four

END OF EXAM #6

ELECTRICIANS PRACTICE EXAMS
JOURNEYMAN ELECTRICIAN
EXAM #7

The following questions are based on the 2011 edition of the National Electrical Code® and are typical of questions encountered on most Journeyman Electricians' Licensing Exams. Select the best answer from the choices given and review your answers with the answer key included in this book.

ALLOTTED TIME: 75 minutes

1. Where multiple ground rods are installed, they shall NOT be spaced less than _____ apart.

A. 2 feet
B. 4 feet
C. 6 feet
D. 8 feet

2. Where a one-family dwelling has a 200 ampere, 120/240 volt, single-phase main service panel and is being supplied with size 2/0 AWG THW copper ungrounded service-entrance conductors in rigid metal conduit (RMC), the MINIMUM allowable size of the bonding jumper for this service-entrance conduit is _____ copper.

A. 6 AWG
B. 4 AWG
C. 2 AWG
D. 1/0 AWG

3. A disconnect switch enclosure installed in a Class II, Div. 2 location shall be _____.

A. dust tight
B. heavy duty type
C. rain tight
D. general duty type

4. The interior of enclosures or raceways installed underground shall be considered to be a _____ location.

A. dry
B. damp
C. hazardous
D. wet

5. Determine the MAXIMUM allowable current-carrying capacity of four (4) size 1/0 AWG THW copper current-carrying conductors installed in a common raceway with an ambient temperature of 86 degrees F.

A. 150 amperes
B. 105 amperes
C. 112 amperes
D. 120 amperes

6. The NEC® defines a continuous load to be a load where the maximum current on the circuit is expected to continue for at LEAST_____ hours or more.

A. three
B. four
C. six
D. eight

7. Determine the MINIMUM size THW copper branch-circuit conductors the NEC® requires to supply a 3-phase, continuous-duty, ac motor that draws 70 amperes per phase. Consider all terminations are rated for 75 deg. C.

A. 1 AWG
B. 2 AWG
C. 3 AWG
D. 4 AWG

8. Given: You have determined a conductor has a computed allowable ampacity of 75 amperes. What is the MAXIMUM standard ampere rating of the overcurrent protection device the NEC® permits to protect this circuit where this is not a motor circuit or part of a multioutlet branch circuit supplying more than one receptacle?

A. 70 amperes
B. 75 amperes
C. 80 amperes
D. 85 amperes

9. A 208-volt, 3-phase, 50 hp, squirrel-cage, continuous-duty, ac motor has a full-load running current rating of _____ .

A. 130 amperes
B. 143 amperes
C. 162 amperes
D. 195 amperes

10. What is the MAXIMUM distance that a disconnect switch is permitted to be located from the operator's station for a portable carnival ride?

A. 6 feet
B. 10 feet
C. 25 feet
D. 50 feet

11. Determine the MINIMUM trade size electrical metallic tubing (EMT) required to enclose eight (8) size 6 AWG copper conductors with THHW insulation, when installed in a 50 foot conduit run.

A. 1 in.
B. 1¼ in.
C. 1½ in.
D. 2 in.

12. Where exceptions are not applicable, when a feeder supplies a continuous load of 240 amperes, the overcurrent protection device protecting this circuit shall have a rating of at LEAST _____ .

A. 240 amperes
B. 300 amperes
C. 250 amperes
D. 275 amperes

13. Liquidtight flexible metal conduit (LFMC) shall be securely fastened WITHIN _____ of each box or other conduit termination.

A. 4½ feet
B. 3 feet
C. 12 inches
D. 18 inches

14. When a pull box contains conductors of size 4 AWG and larger and a straight pull of the conductors is to be made, the length of the box shall NOT be less than _____ times the trade diameter of the largest conduit entering the box.

A. six
B. four
C. eight
D. twelve

15. Conduit nipples not over 24 inches long may be filled to a MAXIMUM of _____ of their cross-sectional area.

A. 30 percent
B. 40 percent
C. 54 percent
D. 60 percent

16. Determine the MAXIMUM number of size 14 AWG THHN conductors permitted to be installed in a trade size 3/8 in. flexible metal conduit (FMC) that contains a bare size 14 AWG grounding conductor, when the FMC has external fittings.

A. two
B. three
C. four
D. five

17. Which of the following listed conduits does the NEC® permit to enclose conductors supplying wet-niche underwater pool luminaires?

A. electrical metallic tubing (EMT)
B. electrical nonmetallic tubing (ENT)
C. galvanized rigid metal conduit (RMC)
D. Schedule 40 rigid polyvinyl chloride conduit (PVC)

18. Underground wiring is not permitted under a permanently installed swimming pool or within _____ of the pool, unless the wiring is supplying the associated pool equipment.

A. 10 feet
B. 6 feet
C. 5 feet
D. 8 feet

19. Which of the following listed types of batteries is NOT permitted for use as a source of power for emergency systems?

A. automotive
B. lead acid type
C. alkali type
D. all of these

20. In new installations, the MINIMUM working space the NEC® requires between a 480Y/277 volt, switchboard and a 480-volt motor control center when facing each other is _____.

A. 3 feet
B. 3½ feet
C. 4 feet
D. 6 feet

21. In guest rooms of hotels, motels, and sleeping rooms of dorms a MINIMUM of _____ general purpose receptacles installed in the room is/are required to be readily accessible.

A. one
B. two
C. three
D. all

22. When branch circuit conductors are installed inside a ballast enclosure and within three (3) inches of the ballast, the conductors shall have a temperature rating NOT lower than _____ .

A. 105 deg. C
B. 90 deg. C
C. 75 deg. C
D. 60 deg. C

23. When a size 4 AWG or larger conductor enters a panelboard, which of the following must be provided?

A. A bonding jumper.
B. A grounding clip.
C. An insulated bushing.
D. An insulated grounding conductor.

24. Class _____ locations are those that are hazardous because of the presence of easily ignitible fibers or where materials producing combustible flyings are handled, but in which such fibers/flyings are not likely to be in suspension in the air in quantites sufficient to produce ignitible mixtures.

A. I
B. II
C. III
D. IV

25. A single-phase, 240-volt, 15 kVA standby generator may be loaded to a MAXIMUM of _____ per line.

A. 62.50 amperes
B. 31.25 amperes
C. 41.66 amperes
D. 52.50 amperes

END OF EXAM #7

ELECTRICIANS PRACTICE EXAMS
JOURNEYMAN ELECTRICIAN
EXAM #8

The following questions are based on the 2011 edition of the National Electrical Code® and are typical of questions encountered on most Journeyman Electricians' Licensing Exams. Select the best answer from the choices given and review your answers with the answer key included in this book.

ALLOTTED TIME: 75 minutes

1. All motors shall be considered as _____ unless the nature of the apparatus it drives is such that the motor will not operate continuously.

A. continuous duty
B. short-time duty
C. intermittent duty
D. periodic duty

2. Where the motor controller also serves as a disconnecting means, it shall open all _____ conductors to the motor.

A. grounded
B. neutral
C. grounding
D. ungrounded

3. Before demand factors are taken into consideration for commercial buildings, general-purpose receptacle loads are to be computed at NOT less than _____ per outlet.

A. 100 VA
B. 120 VA
C. 150 VA
D. 180 VA

4. Conductors with _____ insulation have a greater ampacity when used in a dry location compared to when used in a wet location.

A. THW
B. RHW
C. THWN
C. THHW

5. Where a submersible pump is used in a metal well casing, the well casing shall be _____ the pump circuit equipment grounding conductor.

A. isolated from
B. connected to
C. exothermic welded to
D. none of these

6. In a health care facility, low voltage electrical equipment that is likely to become energized that is frequently in contact with the bodies of patients, shall operate on a voltage of _____ or less if the equipment is not approved as intrinsically safe, double insulated or moisture resistant.

A. 10 volts
B. 24 volts
C. 100 volts
D. 120 volts

7. When ambient temperature is not a factor, a size 8 AWG single copper conductor with type FEPB insulation, installed in free air, will have a MAXIMUM allowable ampacity of _____.

A. 80 amperes
B. 55 amperes
C. 45 amperes
D. 83 amperes

8. For the purpose of determining conductor fill in a device box, a switch is counted as equal to _____ conductor(s), based on the largest conductor connected to the switch.

A. zero
B. one
C. two
D. three

9. When determining the required ampacity of the branch circuit conductors to supply a 3-phase, continuous duty ac motor, current values given on _____ shall be used.

A. the motors nameplate
B. Tbl. 430.248 of the NEC®
C. Tbl. 430.52 of the NEC®
D. Tbl. 430.250 of the NEC®

10. When calculating the total load for a building or structure, what is the MINIMUM computed branch circuit load, in volt-amps, permitted by the NEC® for a branch circuit serving an exterior electric sign?

A. 1,200 volt amps
B. 1,800 volt amps
C. 1,500 volt amps
D. 2,000 volt amps

11. Determine the MAXIMUM number of size 1 AWG XHHW compact conductors permitted in a trade size 3 in., rigid Schedule 40 PVC conduit more than 24 inches long.

A. 21
B. 19
C. 14
D. 18

12. Infrared commercial and industrial heating appliances shall have overcurrent protection NOT exceeding _____.

A. 20 amperes
B. 40 amperes
C. 50 amperes
D. 60 amperes

13. Class _____ hazardous locations are those in which flammable liquid-produced vapors, or combustible liquid-produced vapors are or may be present in the air in quantities sufficient to produce explosive or ignitible mixtures.

A. I
B. II
C. III
D. IV

14. In indoor areas where walls are frequently washed, such as laundries or car washes, metallic conduit and metallic panelboards shall be mounted with a _____ space between the wall and conduit or panelboard when the equipment is installed exposed.

A. 3/4 in.
B. 1/2 in.
C. 1/8 in.
D. 1/4 in.

A branch circuit served by size 12 AWG conductors is a _____ rated branch circuit when protected by a 15-ampere circuit breaker.

A. 20 ampere
B. 25 ampere
C. 15 ampere
D. 10 ampere

16. What is the MAXIMUM overcurrent protection allowed for the protection of resistance-type electric space heating equipment?

A. 30 amperes
B. 40 amperes
C. 48 amperes
D. 60 amperes

17. Information technology equipment shall be permitted to be connected to a branch circuit by a listed power-supply cord having a length NOT to exceed _____.

A. 10 feet
B. 15 feet
C. 12 feet
D. 20 feet

18. Type MI cable shall be supported at intervals NOT exceeding _____.

A. 2 feet
B. 4 feet
C. 6 feet
D. 10 feet

19. The internal depth of an outlet box used to splice conductors to a luminaire shall NOT be less than _____ .

A. 1/2 in.
B. 15/16 in.
C. 3/4 in.
D. 1 in.

20. Direct-buried conductors emerging from grade shall be protected by raceways or covers up to at LEAST _____ above finished grade.

A. 8 feet
B. 10 feet
C. 12 feet
D. 15 feet

21. What is the MINIMUM size equipment grounding conductor for a 50 ampere branch circuit as required by the NEC®?

A. 12 AWG
B. 10 AWG
C. 8 AWG
D. 6 AWG

22. Disregarding exceptions, all 3-phase, 4-wire, 480Y/277 volt, electrical services, require ground-fault protection for each service disconnecting means, when rated for at LEAST _____ or more.

A. 400 amperes
B. 600 amperes
C. 1,000 amperes
D. 1,500 amperes

23. Determine the conductor ampacity given the following related information:

   conductors are size 500 kcmil copper
   conductor insulation is THWN
   eight (8) current-carrying conductors are in the raceway
   ambient temperature is 125 deg. F
   conduit length is 50 feet
   installation is a wet location

   A. 178.2 amperes
   B. 199.5 amperes
   C. 294.6 amperes
   D. 380.0 amperes

24. When connecting to luminaires, trade size 3/8 in. flexible metal conduit (FMC) is permitted to enclose tap conductors, provided the length of the FMC does NOT exceed _____ .

   A. 3 feet
   B. 4 feet
   C. 6 feet
   D. 8 feet

25. Where a trade size 1/2 in. rigid metal conduit (RMC) is installed in a Class I location and a 1/2 in. conduit seal is required, the MINIMUM thickness of the sealing compound shall NOT be less than _____.

   A. 3/8 in.
   B. 1/2 in.
   C. 5/8 in.
   D. 3/4 in.

END OF EXAM #8

…

ELECTRICIANS PRACTICE EXAMS
JOURNEYMAN ELECTRICIAN
EXAM #9

The following questions are based on the 2011 edition of the National Electrical Code® and are typical of questions encountered on most Journeyman Electricians' Licensing Exams. Select the best answer from the choices given and review your answers with the answer key included in this book.

ALLOTTED TIME: 75 minutes

1. Current-carrying conductors installed within electrical nonmetallic tubing (ENT) may carry a MAXIMUM of _____ .

A. 300 volts
B. 450 volts
C. 500 volts
D. 600 volts

2. A 30 hp, 480-volt, 3-phase wound-rotor, ac motor has a full-load running current rating of _____ .

A. 27 amperes
B. 32 amperes
C. 40 amperes
D. 50 amperes

3. The MAXIMUM ampacity of an individual branch circuit in a flat conductor cable assembly shall be _____.

A. 10 amperes
B. 15 amperes
C. 20 amperes
D. 30 amperes

4. When conductors of different systems are installed in the same raceway, one system grounded conductor shall be white or gray. The other system grounded conductor shall be _____ .

A. green only
B. white with an identifying colored stripe that is green
C. white or gray with an identifying colored stripe that is not green
D. white only

5. What MAXIMUM percent of a metal wireway cross-section may be occupied by splices, taps and conductors at any point?

A. 20 percent
B. 30 percent
C. 40 percent
D. 75 percent

6. In an underground rigid polyvinyl chloride conduit (PVC) system that consist of 50 feet length between pulling points, what is the MAXIMUM number of bends this run may have?

A. four (4) - 90 degree
B. six (6) - 90 degree
C. four (4) - 120 degree
D. two (2) - 90 degree

7. Grounding electrodes made of pipe or conduit shall NOT be smaller than _____ electrical trade size.

A. 1/2 in.
B. 3/4 in.
C. 1 in.
D. 1½ in.

8. Liquidtight flexible metallic conduit (LFMC) shall NOT be used:

A. in lengths in excess of 6 feet.
B. in concealed work.
C. in hazardous locations.
D. where subject to physical damage.

9. Determine the allowable ampacity of a size 3 AWG THHN copper conductor where given the following related information.

   Two (2) current-carrying conductors are in the raceway.
   The ambient temperature is 35 deg. C.
   The terminations are rated at 60 deg. C.

A. 105.6 amperes
B. 85 amperes
C. 81.6 amperes
D. 110 amperes

10. In general, communications wires and cables shall have a vertical clearance of NOT less than _____ from all points above roofs which they pass.

A. 3 feet
B. 4 feet
C. 6 feet
D. 8 feet

11. Standard trade size 2 in. rigid Schedule 40 polyvinyl chloride conduit (PVC), shall be supported at LEAST every _____.

A. 3 feet
B. 5 feet
C. 6 feet
D. 8 feet

12. For an ac system operating at less than 1000 volts, a main bonding jumper shall connect the grounded conductor(s) to _____.

A. each service disconnecting means enclosure
B. each meter base only
C. the grounding electrode
D. all sub-panels

13. In industrial establishments, where sizes 1/0 AWG through 4/0 AWG single conductor cables are installed in ladder type cable tray, the MAXIMUM allowable rung spacing for the cable tray shall be _____ .

A. 6 inches
B. 9 inches
C. 12 inches
D. 15 inches

14. The NEC® mandates the MAXIMUM length permitted for a flexible cord supplying a 208-volt, single-phase, room air-conditioner to be _____ .

A. 4 feet
B. 6 feet
C. 8 feet
D. 10 feet

15. In general, which of the following receptacle outlets in a commercial kitchen are required by the NEC® to be GFCI protected?

A. All 125-volt, 15- or 20-ampere receptacles.
B. All 125-volt, 15- or 20-ampere receptacles in wet locations only.
C. All receptacles.
D. All 125-volt countertop receptacles only.

16. Determine the resistance, in ohms, of a 100 watt, 120-volt, incandescent light bulb.

A. 0.833 ohms
B. 1.2 ohms
C. 100 ohms
D. 144 ohms

17. Branch-circuit conductors supplying more than one motor shall have an ampacity of at LEAST_____ of the FLC of the largest motor in the group, and 100 percent of the FLC of the other motor(s) in the group.

A. 25 percent
B. 80 percent
C. 100 percent
D. 125 percent

18. What is the MINIMUM size equipment grounding conductor required for a 5 hp, 3-phase, 208-volt motor having 20 ampere rated overload protection and branch-circuit, short-circuit and ground-fault protection rated 30 amperes?

A. 10 AWG
B. 14 AWG
C. 12 AWG
D. 8 AWG

19. If a circuit breaker serves as the controller for a motor, and the motor is not in sight of the breaker, the NEC® requires which of the following?

A. The motor to be less than 2 hp.
B. The breaker be able to be locked in the open position.
C. The motor to be Code letter "E".
D. The breaker to be rated 25,000 AIC.

20. Equipment grounding conductors in the assured equipment grounding conductor program, shall be tested for continuity and shall be:

A. stranded.
B. copper.
C. electrically continuous.
D. shielded.

21. Where an ac electrical service is supplied with four (4) parallel sets of size 500 kcmil aluminum ungrounded conductors, what is the MINIMUM size copper grounding electrode conductor required when connected to the concrete encased reinforcing building steel?

A. 3/0 AWG
B. 4/0 AWG
C. 250 kcmil
D. 2/0 AWG

22. Where an ac transformer arc welder has a 50 ampere rated primary current and a 60 percent duty cycle, the MINIMUM size 60 deg. C rated copper conductors the NEC® requires to supply this welder is _____ .

A. 6 AWG
B. 8 AWG
C. 10 AWG
D. 4 AWG

23. When installing wiring for sensitive electronic equipment, the MAXIMUM voltage to ground is required to be _____ .

A. 277 volts
B. 120 volts
C. 60 volts
D. 30 volts

24. In a health care facility, a patient bed location in a critical care area is required to have which of the following?

A. Four single receptacles or two duplex receptacles.
B. Six single receptacles or three duplex receptacles.
C. Two duplex receptacles or four single receptacles.
D. Two single receptacles or one duplex receptacle.

25. Flexible cords and cables shall NOT be used _____ .

A. as elevator cables
B. when run through holes in walls
C. as data processing cables
D. to prevent transmission of vibration

END OF EXAM #9

ELECTRICIANS PRACTICE EXAMS
JOURNEYMAN ELECTRICIAN
EXAM #10

The following questions are based on the 2011 edition of the National Electrical Code® and are typical of questions encountered on most Journeyman Electricians' Licensing Exams. Select the best answer from the choices given and review your answers with the answer key included in this book.

ALLOTTED TIME: 75 minutes

1. Electrically heated floors in bathrooms, kitchens, and in hydromassage bathtub locations shall be _____.

A. GFCI protected
B. AFCI protected
C. grounded
D. isolated

2. Which of the following methods is an acceptable marking for the grounding pole on a grounding type receptacle?

A. A green colored hexagonal headed or shaped terminal screw.
B. An orange dot.
C. A white colored round headed screw.
D. An orange colored hexagonal headed screw.

3. What is the MAXIMUM length of a flexible cord that may be used for a recirculating motor on a swimming pool at a dwelling?

A. 3 feet
B. 4 feet
C. 6 feet
D. 8 feet

4. Plate grounding electrodes shall be installed NOT less than _____ below the surface of the earth.

A. 12 inches
B. 18 inches
C. 24 inches
D. 30 inches

5. A disconnecting means shall be provided on the supply side of all fuses in circuits having a voltage of at LEAST _____ to ground.

A. 120 volts
B. 250 volts
C. 150 volts
D. 277 volts

6. Where an 80-ampere, 240-volt, single-phase load is located 200 feet from a panelboard and is supplied with size 3 AWG copper conductors with THWN insulation, what is the approximate voltage-drop on the circuit?
(K = 12.9)

A. 6.0 volts
B. 4.0 volts
C. 9.2 volts
D. 7.84 volts

7. Enclosures in a Class I, Division 1 location containing components that have arcing devices must have an approved seal located within at LEAST _____ of each conduit run entering or leaving such enclosures.

A. 12 inches
B. 18 inches
C. 24 inches
D. 4½ feet

8. According to the NEC® which of the following statements is true about installing listed or labeled equipment?

A. The equipment may be installed in whatever manner the contractor determines best.
B. The equipment shall be installed in accordance with the instructions.
C. The equipment only needs to be listed or labeled if it is installed in an industrial environment.
D. The equipment may be subject to listed or labeled equipment if it is determined to be acceptable by the contractor.

9. The NEC® considers the area around the motor fuel dispensing pumps of a service station to be a hazardous location. This area extends a height of 18 inches above grade, and up to a distance from the enclosure of the outdoor motor fuel dispensing pumps of _____.

A. 5 feet
B. 10 feet
C. 16 feet
D. 20 feet

10. According to the National Electrical Code®, what are the two (2) mandatory branches of the hospital emergency system?

A. The emergency branch and the standby branch.
B. The life safety branch and the critical branch.
C. The normal branch and the alternate branch.
D. The essential branch and the non-essential branch.

11. Class 3 single conductors shall NOT be smaller than _____.

A. 18 AWG
B. 16 AWG
C. 14 AWG
D. 20 AWG

12. Where an office building has a 208Y/120 Volt, 3-phase service with a balanced net computed load of 90 kVA, what is the current each ungrounded (phase) conductor will carry at full load?

A. 188 amperes
B. 250 amperes
C. 433 amperes
D. 750 amperes

13. When grounding the structural reinforcing steel of a swimming pool, what is the smallest size grounding conductor permitted for this installation?

A. 12 AWG
B. 10 AWG
C. 8 AWG
D. 6 AWG

14. When conductors or cables are installed in circular conduits exposed to direct sunlight on or above a rooftop and within at LEAST _____ of the rooftop, a temperature adder must be applied to the applicable correction factors of Table 310.15(B)(2)(a) to determine the allowable ampacity of the conductors.

A. 6 inches
B. 12 inches
C. 24 inches
D. 36 inches

15. Where a motor of more than 1 horsepower has a temperature rise of 50 deg. C indicated on the nameplate, for the purposes of selecting the overload device, this device shall be selected to trip at NO more than _____ of the **motor's full**-load ampere rating. (Assume modification of this value is not necessary.)

A. 100 percent
B. 115 percent
C. 125 percent
D. 130 percent

16. Where a size 14 AWG branch-circuit conductor protected by a 15 ampere rated circuit breaker supplies three (3) 20 ampere rated duplex receptacles, this branch circuit _____ .

A. would be in compliance with the NEC® if the wire was size 12 AWG
B. would be in compliance with the NEC® if the breaker was rated 20-amperes
C. is not in compliance with the NEC® because the receptacles have a 20 ampere rating
D. is in compliance with the NEC®

17. What is the MAXIMUM number of times a grounding electrode conductor is permitted to be spliced by use of listed split-bolt connectors?

A. one
B. two
C. three
D. none

18. Given: A metal junction box has a volume of 27 cubic inches and contains a total of six (6) size 12 AWG conductors, no grounding conductors, devices or fittings are contained in the box. Additional wires of size 10 AWG need to be added in the box. What is the MAXIMUM number of size 10 AWG conductors may be added to this box?

A. two
B. five
C. six
D. eight

19. For enclosing a mobile home supply cord, what is the MAXIMUM trade size conduit permitted between the branch circuit panelboard of a mobile home and the underside of a mobile home floor?

A. 1 in.
B. 1¼ in.
C. 1½ in.
D. 2 in.

20. Which of the following wiring methods is/are approved for use for fixed wiring in an area above Class I locations in a commercial garage?

A. Type MI cable
B. Type TC cable
C. Type MC cable
D. all of the above

21. Class II locations are those that are hazardous because of the presence of _____ .

A. flammable gas
B. ignitible fibers
C. ignitible vapors
D. combustible dust

22. Branch-circuit conductors supplying a fixed storage-type electric water heater with a capacity of 120 gallons or less, shall have an ampacity of NOT less than _____ of the full-load current of the water heater.

A. 80 percent
B. 100 percent
C. 125 percent
D. 150 percent

23. Household-type appliances with surface heating elements having a MAXIMUM demand of more than _____ shall have its power supply subdivided into two (2) or more circuits.

A. 60 amperes
B. 50 amperes
C. 40 amperes
D. 30 amperes

24. When driving a ground rod and solid rock is encountered, the ground rod is permitted to be buried in a trench at LEAST _____ deep.

A. 3 feet
B. 4 feet
C. 24 inches
D. 30 inches

25. A total of ten (10) copper THW conductors are to be installed in a 20 foot run of intermediate metal conduit (IMC), five (5) size 1 AWG and five (5) size 3 AWG. What is the MINIMUM allowable trade size IMC required to contain these ten (10) conductors?

A. 1½ in.
B. 2 in.
C. 2½ in.
D. 3 in.

END OF EXAM #10

ELECTRICIANS PRACTICE EXAMS
JOURNEYMAN ELECTRICIAN
EXAM #11

The following questions are based on the 2011 edition of the National Electrical Code® and are typical of questions encountered on most Journeyman Electricians' Licensing Exams. Select the best answer from the choices given and review your answers with the answer key included in this book.

ALLOTTED TIME: 75 minutes

1. Where flexible cord is used as the wiring method to supply ac motors, the MINIMUM size of the conductors shall be selected in accordance with _____ of the NEC®.

A. Table 310.15(B)(16)
B. Table 310.15(B)(17)
C. Table 310.15(B)(18)
D. Section 400.5

2. When an industrial control panel is supplied from a 3-phase, 4-wire, delta-connected electrical system, the phase having the higher voltage to ground is _____ .

A. required to be the "A" phase
B. required to be the "B" phase
C. required to be the "C" phase
D. permitted to be any phase

3. When conductors having a voltage of not more than 600 volts pass above a public driveway, they shall have a MINIMUM clearance of NOT less than _____ above finished grade.

A. 10 feet
B. 15 feet
C. 18 feet
D. 20 feet

4. Shore power for boats shall be provided by single receptacles rated NOT less than _____ .

A. 20 amperes
B. 30 amperes
C. 50 amperes
D. 60 amperes

5. Where a mobile home has the main service disconnecting means installed outdoors, the disconnecting means shall be installed so the bottom of the enclosure is NOT less than _____ above finished grade.

A. two feet
B. three feet
C. four feet
D. six feet

6. Determine the MAXIMUM allowable ampacity of a 3-conductor size 6 AWG XHHW aluminum SER cable installed in the attic of a one-family dwelling where the ambient temperature is 44 degrees C.

A. 41.2 amperes
B. 52.2 amperes
C. 47.9 amperes
D. 56.2 amperes

7. Unless specifically identified for a higher percentage of fill, the cross-sectional area of the conductors in a conduit seal shall NOT exceed _____ of the cross-sectional area of a rigid metal conduit of the same trade size.

A. 25 percent
B. 40 percent
C. 50 percent
D. 60 percent

8. Storage batteries in a solar photovoltaic system shall be provided with a MINIMUM workspace depth of NOT less than _____.

A. 24 inches
B. 30 inches
C. 36 inches
D. 42 inches

9. Direct-buried cables or conductors located in a trench below two (2) inch thick concrete or equivalent shall have a MINIMUM cover requirement of _____.

A. 6 inches
B. 12 inches
C. 18 inches
D. 24 inches

10. The MAXIMUM unsupported length of Type MC cable used to supply a luminaire in an accessible ceiling is permitted to be NOT more than _____ in length.

A. 10 feet
B. 6 feet
C. 4½ feet
D. 18 inches

11. Which of the following listed is/are prohibited from being supplied through AFCI or GFCI protective devices?

A. 120-volt smoke alarms
B. fire alarm systems
C. 120-volt receptacle outlets in residential garages
D. residential lighting outlets

12. Where a submersible pump is located in a pond of a water treatment plant, the on land service equipment for the pump shall be NO closer than _____ horizontally from the shoreline.

A. 6 feet
B. 10 feet
C. 5 feet
D. 3 feet

13. When splicing existing underground service conductors to extend to a new service location, the NEC® requires _____ .

   I. the use of splice boxes
   II. the conductors to be protected with a covering of at least two (2) inches of concrete

   A. I only
   B. II only
   C. either I or II
   D. neither I nor II

14. Equipment supplied by Class 1 circuits such as fire alarm, control, and signaling circuits shall be grounded, UNLESS operating at less than _____ .

   A. 25 volts
   B. 120 volts
   C. 50 volts
   D. 150 volts

15. A single-phase, 120/240 volt, 18 kW rated home standby generator has a full-load current rating of _____ .

   A. 75 amperes
   B. 87 amperes
   C. 100 amperes
   D. 150 amperes

16. A premises wiring system supplied by a grounded ac electrical service, shall have a grounding electrode conductor connected to _____ .

   A. the grounded service conductor
   B. the service disconnect enclosure
   C. the equipment grounding conductor
   D. the meter socket enclosure

17. Intrinsically safe apparatus, associated apparatus, and other equipment shall be installed _____, unless the equipment is a simple apparatus that does not interconnect intrinsically safe circuits.

A. in accordance with the control drawings
B. in the electrical equipment room
C. on a backboard of at least 3/4 in. thick plywood
D. in a dedicated enclosure

18. When a retail furniture store has 80 continuous linear feet of display show window, the NEC® mandates at LEAST _____ receptacle outlets be provided within 18 inches of the top of the show window for the show window lighting.

A. six
B. seven
C. eight
D. nine

19. An inverter or an ac module in an interactive solar photovoltaic system shall _____ upon loss of voltage from the local utility company.

A. continue to operate
B. automatically de-energize its output
C. not operate as a stand alone system
D. be required to be manually reset before re-energized

20. What MINIMUM size 75°C copper feeder conductors are required to supply the following listed 3-phase, 230-volt motors?

    one (1) 15 hp wound-rotor
    one (1) 7½ hp induction-type
    one (1) 3 hp induction-type

A. 4 AWG THWN
B. 4 AWG THHN
C. 3 AWG THW
D. 2 AWG THW

21. Which of the following is NOT required to be marked on the nameplate of a transformer?

A. kVA rating
B. manufacturer
C. voltage
D. overcurrent protection

22. In general, when current-carrying conductors are installed in parallel, the paralleled conductors in each phase shall _____.

   I. be the same size in circular mil area
   have the same insulation type

A. I only
B. II only
C. both I and II
D. neither I nor II

23. When determining the allowable ampacity of conductors where the conductors or cables are installed in conduits exposed to direct sunlight four (4) inches above a rooftop, a temperature value of _____ shall be added to the expected outdoor ambient temperature to determine the applicable correction factors of Table 310.15(B)(2)(a).

A. 60 degrees F
B. 40 degrees F
C. 30 degrees F
D. 25 degrees F

24. Where transformer vaults are not protected with an automatic fire-suppression system, they shall be constructed of materials that have a MINIMUM fire-resistance rating of _____.

A. 1 hour
B. 2 hours
C. 3 hours
D. 4 hours

25. In regard to new outdoor installations of permanently installed swimming pools, luminaires installed above the pool or within 5 feet horizontally from the inside wall of the pool, shall be installed at a height of NOT less than _____ above the maximum water level of the pool.

A. 10 feet
B. 12 feet
C. 15 feet
D. 8 feet

END OF EXAM #11

ELECTRICIANS PRACTICE EXAMS
MASTER ELECTRICIAN
EXAM #12

The following questions are based on the 2011 edition of the National Electrical Code® and are typical of questions encountered on most Master Electricians' Licensing Exams. Select the best answer from the choices given and review your answers with the answer key included in this book.

ALLOTTED TIME: 75 minutes

1. For solar photovoltaic systems, locating the system grounding connection point as close as practicable to the photovoltaic source better protects the system from _____.

A. voltage surges due to ground-faults
B. excessive voltage-drop
C. voltage surges due to lightning
D. excessive resistance in the grounding system

2. What is the MINIMUM height allowed for a fence enclosing an outdoor installation of 2,400 volt electrical equipment?

A. 6 feet
B. 7 feet
C. 8 feet
D. 9 feet

3. Where power for equipment is directly associated with the radio frequency distribution system is carried by the coaxial cable, and the power source is a power limiting transformer, what is the MAXIMUM voltage this coaxial cable may carry?

A. 50 volts
B. 60 volts
C. 120 volts
D. 150 volts

4. Where a 15-ampere rated general-use ac snap switch is used as a disconnecting means for an ac motor, the NEC® requires the MAXIMUM full-load current rating of the motor to be NO more than _____ .

A. 7.5 amperes
B. 10 amperes
C. 12 amperes
D. 15 amperes

Determine the MAXIMUM number of 125-volt, general-purpose receptacles the NEC® permits to be protected by a 20-ampere, 120-volt, single-pole inverse time circuit breaker in a commercial occupancy.

A. 18
B. 15
C. 13
D. 10

6. Which of the following statements, if any, is/are true regarding illumination for service equipment installed in electrical equipment rooms?

The illumination shall not be controlled by means of three way switches.
II. The illumination shall not be controlled by automatic means only.

A. I only
B. II only
C. both I and II
D. neither I nor II

7. In regard to the tenant spaces in a retail shopping mall; each occupant shall have access to the main disconnecting means, EXCEPT:

A. where the service and maintenance are provided by the building management.
B. where there are more than six disconnecting means provided.
C. where the primary feeder transformer does not exceed 600 volts.
D. where the secondary of the service transformer does not exceed 240-volts to ground.

8. Determine the conductor allowable ampacity given the following conditions:

ambient temperature of 44 deg. C
250 kcmil THWN copper conductors
four (4) current-carrying conductors are in the raceway
length of raceway is 25 feet

A. 160 amperes
B. 167 amperes
C. 200 amperes
D. 209 amperes

9. Determine the MAXIMUM overcurrent protection permitted for size THWN copper motor control circuit conductors tapped from the load side of a motor overcurrent protection device. Given: the conductors require short-circuit protection and do not extend beyond the motor control equipment enclosure.

A. 20 amperes
B. 25 amperes
C. 30 amperes
D. 100 amperes

10. Circuit breakers rated _____ or less and 600 volts or less shall have the ampere rating molded, stamped, etched or similarly marked into their handles or escutcheon areas.

A. 600 amperes
B. 200 amperes
C. 400 amperes
D. 100 amperes

11. Where a grounding ring consist of size 2 AWG bare copper wire encircling a building, buried 36 inches, in direct contact with the earth, what is the MINIMUM length of the wire permitted for the grounding electrode in this ground ring?

A. 15 feet
B. 20 feet
C. 25 feet
D. 50 feet

Copyright© 2016

12. Where a rooftop mounted air-conditioning unit is supplied with three (3) size 8 AWG THWN copper conductors, enclosed in an electrical metallic tubing (EMT) within three (3) inches of the rooftop, and exposed to direct sunlight and an ambient temperature of 100 degrees F, the allowable ampacity of the conductors is _____ .

A. 50 amperes
B. 44 amperes
C. 29 amperes
D. 25 amperes

13. Which of the following listed conductor insulations is oil resistant?

A. TW
B. TFE
C. THWN
D. MTW

14. All exposed non-current-carrying metal parts of an information technology system shall _____ or shall be double insulated.

A. be bonded to the equipment grounding conductor
B. not be bonded to the equipment grounding conductor
C. be bonded to the grounded conductor
D. be isolated

15. Determine the MINIMUM number of 15-ampere, 120-volt general lighting branch circuits required for a 12,000 square feet multifamily condo where each dwelling unit has cooking facilities provided.

A. 15
B. 20
C. 24
D. 30

16. Storage batteries used as a source of power for emergency systems shall be of a suitable rating and capacity to supply and maintain the total load for at LEAST _____ .

A. 1/2 hour
B. 1 hour
C. 1½ hours
D. 2 hours

17. When a conduit containing service-entrance conductors runs beneath a building, what is the MINIMUM depth of concrete required to cover the conduit for it to be considered "outside" the building?

A. 2 inches
B. 6 inches
C. 12 inches
D. 18 inches

18. The entire area of an aircraft hanger, including any adjacent and communicating areas not suitably cut off from the hanger, shall be classified as a Class I, Division 2 or Zone 2 location up to a level _____ above the floor.

A. 12 inches
B. 18 inches
C. 24 inches
D. 30 inches

19. Where a 240-volt, single-phase 90 ampere load is located 225 feet from a panelboard and supplied with size 3 THWN copper conductors; what is the approximate voltage drop on this circuit? (K = 12.9)

A. 6 volts
B. 4 volts
C. 8 volts
D. 10 volts

20. The continuity of the grounding system for portable electrical carnival equipment shall be verified _____ .

A. and recorded on an annual basis
B. and recorded on a quarterly basis
C. and recorded on a monthly basis
D. each time the equipment is connected

21. Electrical services and feeders for recreational vehicle parks shall be calculated on the basis of NOT less than _____ per RV site equipped with both 20-ampere and 30-ampere supply facilities.

A. 2400 volt-amperes
B. 9600 volt-amperes
C. 4800 volt-amperes
D. 3600 volt-amperes

22. In a commercial garage work area, which of the following receptacles, if any, are required to have GFCI protection?

15-ampere general-purpose receptacles for hand tools and portable lighting equipment.
20-ampere receptacles serving electrical diagnostic equipment only.

A. I only
B. II only
C. both I and II
D. neither I nor II

23. When sizing time-delay Class CC fuses for motor branch-circuit, short-circuit and ground-fault protection, they are to be sized at the same value as _____ .

A. inverse-time circuit breakers
B. nontime-delay fuses
C. instantaneous trip circuit breakers
D. adjustable trip circuit breakers

24. The MINIMUM spacing required between the bottom of a 600 volt rated switchboard and the noninsulated busbars mounted in the switchboard cabinet is _____ .

A. 6 inches
B. 8 inches
C. 10 inches
D. 12 inches

25. Given: A rigid metal conduit (RMC) to be installed will contain only the following three (3) circuits on the load side of the service overcurrent protective devices:

two - 150 ampere, 3-phase circuits
one - 300 ampere, single-phase circuit

The load side equipment bonding jumper for this conduit must be a MINIMUM size of _____ copper.

A. 1 AWG
B. 2 AWG
C. 4 AWG
D. 6 AWG

END OF EXAM #12

ELECTRICIANS PRACTICE EXAMS
MASTER ELECTRICIAN
EXAM #13

The following questions are based on the 2011 edition of the National Electrical Code® and are typical of questions encountered on most Master Electricians' Licensing Exams. Select the best answer from the choices given and review your answers with the answer key included in this book.

ALLOTTED TIME: 75 minutes

1. Where conduits enter a floor-standing switchboard or panelboard at the bottom, the conduits, including their end fittings, shall NOT rise more than _____ above the bottom of the enclosure.

A. 6 inches
B. 4 inches
C. 2 inches
D. 3 inches

2. Flat conductor cable (FCC) systems may be used in _____.

A. school buildings
B. damp locations
C. hospital buildings
D. None of these

3. Conductors supplying outlets for arc and xenon motion picture projectors of the professional type shall be a MINIMUM size of _____.

A. 12 AWG
B. 10 AWG
C. 8 AWG
D. 6 AWG

4. Thermostatically controlled switching devices serving as both controllers and disconnecting means for fixed electric space heating equipment shall _____.

A. be prohibited
B. be located not more than 5 feet above the floor level
C. directly open all grounded conductors when manually placed in the OFF position
D. be designed so that the circuit cannot be energized automatically after the device has been manually placed in the OFF position

5. A bonding jumper connected between the communications grounding electrode and power grounding electrode system at the building or structure service where separate electrodes are used shall NOT be smaller than size _____ copper.

A. 8 AWG
B. 6 AWG
C. 12 AWG
D. 10 AWG

6. Given: A straight pull of size 4 AWG and larger conductors is to made in a junction box that will have a 3 in. conduit and two (2) 2 in. conduits entering on the same side and exiting on the opposite wall. No splices or terminations will be made in the box. Which of the following listed junction boxes is the MINIMUM required for this installation?

A. 18 in. x 12 in.
B. 20 in. x 18 in.
C. 20 in. x 12 in.
D. 24 in. x 24 in.

7. The demand factor of any electrical system is the ratio of the maximum demand for a system to:

A. the total connected load of the system.
B. 125% of the total connected load of the system.
C. 125% of the total connected continuous load of the system.
D. 80% of the total connected non-continuous load plus 125% of the total connected continuous load of the system.

8. All 15- or 20-ampere, single-phase, 125-volt receptacles located within at LEAST _____ of the edge of a decorative fountain shall be provided with GFCI protection for personnel.

A. 10 feet
B. 15 feet
C. 20 feet
D. 25 feet

9. The emergency controls for attended self-service gasoline stations or convenience stores with motor fuel dispensing facilities must be located NOT more than _____ from the motor fuel dispensers.

A. 20 feet
B. 50 feet
C. 75 feet
D. 100 feet

10. Given: A transformer is fed with four (4) parallel size 500 kcmil conductors per phase. The conductors enter the enclosure on the opposite wall of the terminals. What is the MINIMUM wire-bending space required for the conductors?

A. 16 inches
B. 14 inches
C. 12 inches
D. 10 inches

11. What is the MINIMUM size THWN copper conductors required to supply a continuous-duty, 25 hp, 208-volt, 3-phase motor, where the motor is on the end of a short conduit run that contains only three (3) conductors, at an ambient temperature of 115 deg. F?

A. 6 AWG
B. 3 AWG
C. 2 AWG
D. 1 AWG

12. Where time-delay (dual-element) fuses are used for short-circuit and ground-fault protection for both windings of a part-winding synchronous motor, the fuses shall be permitted to have a rating NOT exceeding _____ of the full-load current of the motor.

A. 200 percent
B. 150 percent
C. 175 percent
D. 225 percent

13. Which of the following shall be installed on the critical branch of the emergency system in a health care facility?

A. exit signs
B. nurse call systems
C. communication systems
D. fire alarms

14. Apply the general method of calculation for dwellings and determine the demand load, in kW, on the ungrounded service-entrance conductors for four (4) household electric ranges rated 19 kW each.

A. 34 kW
B. 17 kW
C. 38 kW
D. 23 kW

15. When calculating the service-entrance conductors for a farm service, the second largest load of the total load, shall be calculated at _____ .

A. 90 percent
B. 80 percent
C. 75 percent
D. 65 percent

16. Single-conductor cable Type _____ shall be permitted in exposed outdoor locations in photovoltaic source circuits for photovoltaic module interconnections within the photovoltaic array.

A. UF
B. THHN
C. USE-2
D. THWN

17. What percent of electrical supplied spaces in a recreational vehicle park must be equipped with at least one (1) 30-ampere 125-volt receptacle outlet?

A. 60 percent
B. 70 percent
C. 90 percent
D. 100 percent

18. The collector ring used for grounding of an irrigation machine shall have a current rating of NOT less than _____ of the full-load current of the largest device served plus the sum of the other devices served.

A. 75 percent
B. 80 percent
C. 100 percent
D. 125 percent

19. Where a 3-phase, 25 kVA rated transformer with a 480-volt primary and a 208Y/120 volt secondary is to be installed, and primary and secondary protection is required to be provided, determine the MAXIMUM standard ampere rating of secondary overcurrent protection permitted by the NEC®.

A. 80 amperes
B. 90 amperes
C. 100 amperes
D. 110 amperes

20. Where ungrounded conductors are run in parallel in multiple raceways, the equipment grounding conductor, where used, shall be _____.

A. omitted
B. run in parallel in each raceway
C. installed in one raceway only
D. bare

21. Where track lighting is installed in a continuous row, each individual section of NOT more than _____ in length shall be securely supported.

A. 2 feet
B. 4 feet
C. 6 feet
D. 8 feet

22. Determine the MINIMUM size THWN copper feeder conductors required by the NEC® to supply the following 480 volt, continuous duty, 3-phase, induction-type, Design C, motors.

one - 40 hp
one - 50 hp
one - 60 hp

A. 2/0 AWG
B. 3/0 AWG
C. 4/0 AWG
D. 250 kcmil

23. In health care facilities, essential electrical systems shall have a MINIMUM _____ .

A. of one (1) hour back-up time
B. capacity of 200 gallons of fuel for the auxillary generator
C. of two (2) independent sources of power
D. capacity of 150 kVA

24. Where compressed natural gas vehicles are repaired in a major repair garage, the area within _____ of the ceiling shall be considered unclassified where adequate ventilation is provided.

A. 18 inches
B. 24 inches
C. 30 inches
D. 36 inches

25. Where a 3-phase, 480-volt, 100 ampere demand load is located 390 feet from a panelboard, what MINIMUM size THWN aluminum conductors are required to supply the load, where the voltage drop is required to be limited to 3 percent? (K = 21.2)

A. 2 AWG
B. 1 AWG
C. 1/0 AWG
D. 2/0 AWG

END OF EXAM #13

ELECTRICIANS PRACTICE EXAMS
MASTER ELECTRICIAN
EXAM #14

The following questions are based on the 2011 edition of the National Electrical Code® and are typical of questions encountered on most Master Electricians' Licensing Exams. Select the best answer from the choices given and review your answers with the answer key included in this book.

ALLOTTED TIME: 75 minutes

1. When a portable generator is used for a portable optional standby source and is not considered a separately derived system, the equipment grounding conductor shall be bonded to _____.

A. the generator frame and the grounded conductor
B. the system grounding electrode
C. a grounding electrode only
D. the grounded conductor

2. In general, where a cablebus system is rated 95 amperes, the MAXIMUM allowable rating of the overcurrent device that may be used to protect the cablebus is _____ .

A. 80 amperes
B. 90 amperes
C. 95 amperes
D. 100 amperes

3. A feeder tap less than 25 feet in length is not required to have overcurrent protection if the ampacity of the tap conductors is NOT less than _____ of the rating of the overcurrent device protecting the feeder conductors.

A. one-half
B. one-fourth
C. one-third
D. 75 percent

4. Given: A flexible metal conduit (FMC) to be installed will contain three (3) size 400 kcmil THWN copper conductors and one (1) size 250 kcmil copper conductor. Where the FMC is more than 24 inches long, what MINIMUM trade size FMC is permitted for this installation?

A. 3 in.
B. 3½ in.
C. 2½ in.
D. 4 in.

5. In general, which of the following MUST be provided at a patient bed location used for general care in a hospital?

A. Circuit on normal system.
B. Circuit on emergency system.
C. "Hospital-grade" receptacles.
D. All of these.

6. When an electrical service is required to have a grounded conductor present, what is the smallest grounded conductor permitted for an electric service using size 1000 kcmil copper ungrounded conductors installed in a single raceway?

A. 3/0 copper
B. 2/0 copper
C. 1/0 copper
D. 4/0 copper

7. Determine the MINIMUM number of 20-ampere, 277-volt, general-lighting branch circuits required for a 150,000 square foot retail department store where the actual connected load is 400 kVA; consider circuit breakers of this size are NOT rated for continuous use.

A. 72
B. 82
C. 91
D. 102

8. Where a 2-gang box contains two (2) single-pole switches, unless the box is equipped with permanently installed barriers, voltage between the switches shall NOT be in excess of _____.

A. 120 volts
B. 277 volts
C. 480 volts
D. 240 volts

9. Inverse time circuit breakers that have an interrupting rating other than _____, shall have the interrupting rating indicated on the circuit breaker.

A. 1,000 amperes
B. 5,000 amperes
C. 10,00 amperes
D. 20,000 amperes

10. Fluorescent luminaires installed MORE than _____ above the floor in patient care areas in a hospital, shall NOT be required to be grounded by an insulated equipment grounding conductor.

A. 6 feet
B. 6½ feet
C. 7 feet
D. 7½ feet

11. Where nonmetallic conduit is used to enclose conductors supplying a wet-niche luminaire located in a permanently installed swimming pool, a size _____ insulated copper grounding conductor shall be installed in the conduit, unless a listed low-voltage lighting system not requiring grounding is used.

A. 12 AWG
B. 10 AWG
C. 8 AWG
D. 6 AWG

12. The ampacity of phase conductors from the generator terminals to the first overcurrent device shall NOT be less than _____ of the nameplate current rating of the generator where the design of the generator does not prevent overloading.

A. 100 percent
B. 115 percent
C. 125 percent
D. 150 percent

13. In Class II, Division 1 locations, an approved method of connection of conduit to boxes or cabinets is _____ .

A. compression fittings
B. threaded bosses
C. welding
D. all of these

14. The upward discharging vent of an underground fuel tank of motor fuel dispensing facilities is classified as a Class I, Division 1 location WITHIN _____ of the open vent.

A. 3 feet
B. 5 feet
C. 6 feet
D. 8 feet

15. Conductors between the controller and the diesel engine of a fire pump are required to be _____ .

A. 90 deg. C rated
B. 104 deg. C rated
C. stranded
D. solid

16. The MAXIMUM allowable ampacity of a size 750 kcmil XHHW aluminum conductor when there are six (6) current-carrying conductors all of the same size and insulation in the raceway, installed in a dry location where the ambient temperature will reach 22 deg. C is _____.

A. 323.40 amperes
B. 365.40 amperes
C. 361.92 amperes
D. 348.00 amperes

17. Cable trays are permitted to be installed in all of the following locations, EXCEPT _____.

A. basements
B. storage rooms
C. sealed ceiling spaces
D. when passing through a wall

18. According to the NEC®, flat conductor cable (FCC) is permitted to be used for:

I. general-purpose circuit conductors.
II. appliance circuit conductors.

A. I only
B. II only
C. both I and II
D. neither I nor II

Determine the MINIMUM size USE aluminum cable permitted for use on an underground 120/240 volt, single-phase, service for a small office building that has a total load of 23,600 VA after all demand factors have been taken into consideration. Consider all conductor terminations are rated for 75 deg. C.

A. 1/0 AWG
B. 2/0 AWG
C. 1 AWG
D. 2 AWG

20. For track lighting installed in a retail store, a MAXIMUM of two (2) feet of lighting track or fraction thereof shall be considered _____.

A. 150 VA
B. 180 VA
C. 200 VA
D. 100 VA

21. Where an apartment complex has a connected lighting load of 205.4 kVA, what is the demand load, in kVA, on the ungrounded service-entrance conductors? Consider each apartment unit has provisions for cooking by tenants and apply the general (standard) method of calculation for dwelling units.

A. 60.2 kVA
B. 16.5 kVA
C. 63.0 kVA
D. 65.3 kVA

22. All of the following copper conductors are to be installed in an electrical metallic tubing (EMT) ten (10) feet long:

  24 - size 10 AWG THHW
  10 - size 10 AWG THHN
  14 - size 12 AWG THHN

Determine the MINIMUM trade size EMT required.

A. 2 in.
B. 2½ in.
C. 3 in.
D. 3½ in.

23. Given: A 40 unit apartment complex with a 120/240 volt, single-phase electrical system is to add a 6,000 watt, 240 volt, single-phase clothes dryer in each unit. How many amperes will the clothes dryers add to the ungrounded (line) service-entrance conductors when applying the general method of calculation?

A. 265 amperes
B. 270 amperes
C. 300 amperes
D. 350 amperes

24. When sizing fuses for a branch circuit serving a hermetic refrigerant motor-compressor, the device shall NOT exceed _____ of the rated load current marked on the nameplate of the equipment.

A. 115 percent
B. 125 percent
C. 175 percent
D. 225 percent

25. Given: You are to install 90 feet of multioutlet assembly in the computer lab of a school where the computers are likely to be used simultaneously. Determine the MINIMUM number of 20-ampere, 120-volt, single-phase branch circuits required to supply the multioutlet assembly.

A. six
B. seven
C. eight
D. nine

END OF EXAM #14

ELECTRICIANS PRACTICE EXAMS
MASTER ELECTRICIAN
EXAM #15

The following questions are based on the 2011 edition of the National Electrical Code® and are typical of questions encountered on most Master Electricians' Licensing Exams. Select the best answer from the choices given and review your answers with the answer key included in this book.

ALLOTTED TIME: 75 minutes

1. Overcurrent protection for size 18 AWG non-power-limited fire alarm (NPLFA) circuit conductors shall NOT exceed _____ and the overcurrent protection for size 16 AWG NPLFA circuit conductors shall NOT exceed _____.

A. 8 amperes, 10 amperes
B. 7 amperes, 12 amperes
C. 8 amperes, 12 amperes
D. 7 amperes, 10 amperes

2. The maximum number of conductors allowed in a conduit or tubing shall NOT exceed _____.

A. 40 percent of the cross-sectional area of the conduit
B. 30 percent of the cross-sectional area of the conduit
C. the allowable percentage fill specified in Table 1, Chapter 9 of the NEC®
D. the allowable percentage fill of Table 310.15(B)(3)(a) of the NEC®

3. An emergency system is required to have NO more than, _____ to have power available in the event of failure of the normal supply system.

A. 10 seconds
B. 15 seconds
C. 60 seconds
D. 3 minutes

4. X-ray equipment installed in a hospital may be served by a hard-service cord with a suitable attachment plug, provided the branch circuit rating does NOT exceed _____.

A. 15 amperes
B. 20 amperes
C. 30 amperes
D. 50 amperes

5. Elevator driving motors used with a generator field control are rated as _____ duty motors.

A. intermittent
B. continuous
C. variable
D. controlled

6. Where a direct burial cable has a voltage of 45 kV, the NEC® mandates the MINIMUM burial depth of the cable to be at LEAST _____ .

A. 24 inches
B. 36 inches
C. 42 inches
D. 48 inches

7. Given: A recreational vehicle campground has a total of 150 campsites with electrical power. Twenty-five (25) of the campsites are reserved as tent sites. How many sites are required to have at LEAST one (1) 20 ampere, 125-volt, receptacle outlet?

A. 105
B. 125
C. 150
D. None

8. Determine the MINIMUM size type SO cord permitted to supply a 40 hp, 460-volt, 3-phase, continuous-duty, ac wound rotor, motor installed in an area with an ambient temperature of 86 degrees F.

A. 2 AWG
B. 4 AWG
C. 6 AWG
D. 8 AWG

9. Where a 30 hp, 240-volt, 3-phase synchronous motor has a power factor of 90 percent, as per the NEC® the full-load running current of the motor is _____ .

A. 63.0 amperes
B. 69.3 amperes
C. 76.23 amperes
D. 86.62 amperes

10. When water reaches the height of the established electrical datum plane for an irrigation pond, the service equipment must _____ .

A. be installed in a NEMA 6 enclosure
B. float
C. be installed in a NEMA 6P enclosure
D. disconnect

11. When installing emergency battery pack lighting unit equipment, the branch-circuit feeding this equipment shall:

A. be connected to the nearest receptacle outlet.
B. come from the closest outlet of power that is compatible with the emergency lights rated voltage.
C. be fed only from an identified emergency lighting panel.
D. be on the same branch-circuit serving the normal lighting in the area.

12. In an industrial establishment, what is the MAXIMUM length of 200 ampere rated busway that may be tapped to a 600 ampere rated busway without providing additional overcurrent protection?

A. 10 feet
B. 25 feet
C. 50 feet
D. 75 feet

13. Size 4/0 AWG, 75 deg. C aluminum secondary conductors of a 3-phase delta-wye transformer, shall be protected at NOT more than _____ .

175 amperes
200 amperes
the calculated load connected to the transformer
none of these, because secondary protection is not required for multiphase, delta-wye transformer secondary conductors

14. For trade size 3/4 in. MI cable, the radius of the inner edge of the bend shall NOT be less than _____ times the external diameter of the cable.

A. three
B. four
C. five
D. seven

15. Where a flat cable assembly, Type FC, is installed LESS than _____ above the floor or fixed working platform, it shall be protected by a cover identified for the use.

A. 6 feet
B. 7 feet
C. 8 feet
D. 10 feet

16. The MINIMUM burial depth for conduit or cables installed under an airport runway, concourse or tarmac is _____.

A. 1½ feet
B. 2 feet
C. 3 feet
D. 4 feet

17. Determine the MINIMUM size overload protection required for a 480 volt, 3-phase, 15 hp, continuous-duty motor given the following related information:

Design C
temperature rise - 40 deg. C
service factor - 1.12
actual nameplate rating - 18 amperes

A. 20.7 amperes
B. 18.0 amperes
C. 22.5 amperes
D. 23.4 amperes

18. Assume where the overload protection you have selected on the above motor is not sufficient to start the motor and trips, therefore, modification of this value is necessary, determine the MAXIMUM size overload protection permitted.

A. 22.5 amperes
B. 20.7 amperes
C. 25.2 amperes
D. 23.4 amperes

19. Where a 50 kVA transformer with a 480-volt, 3 phase primary and a 208Y/120 volt, 3-phase secondary is to be installed and overcurrent protection is required on both the primary and secondary side of the transformer; determine the MAXIMUM size overcurrent protection device permitted for the primary side.

A. 125 amperes
B. 150 amperes
C. 175 amperes
D. 200 amperes

20. What is the demand load, in VA, for the general-use receptacles in an office building that has a total of 150 general-use, 125-volt, 20-ampere, single-phase receptacle outlets installed?

A. 18,500 VA
B. 10,000 VA
C. 27,000 VA
D. 13,500 VA

21. Determine the MAXIMUM number of size 12 AWG conductors permitted to be housed in a 3½ in. deep, 3-gang masonry box that contains three (3) switches.

A. 21
B. 23
C. 24
D. 27

22. A horizontal raceway entering a dust-ignition proof enclosure from one that is not, need not have a seal-off if it is at LEAST_____ in length.

A. 18 inches
B. 5 feet
C. 10 feet
D. 25 inches

23. Where abandoned communications cables are identified for future use with a tag, the tag shall be _____.

A. red in color
B. orange in color
C. located outside the junction box
D. of sufficient durability to withstand the environment

24. In a dairy, noncurrent-carrying metal parts of equipment MUST be grounded by _____.

A. an insulated copper equipment grounding conductor
B. a driven ground rod
C. a metal water pipe
D. a grounded conductor

25. A dry type transformer of less than 600 volts and _____ is permitted to be installed in a hollow space of a building, such as above a lift-out ceiling, provided there is adequate ventilation.

A. 25 kVA
B. 37½ kVA
C. 50 kVA
D. 112½ kVA

END OF EXAM #15

ELECTRICIANS PRACTICE EXAMS
MASTER ELECTRICIAN
EXAM #16

The following questions are based on the 2011 edition of the National Electrical Code® and are typical of questions encountered on most Master Electricians' Licensing Exams. Select the best answer from the choices given and review your answers with the answer key included in this book.

ALLOTTED TIME: 75 minutes

1. In Class II, Division 1 locations, where pendant mounted luminaires are suspended by rigid metal conduit (RMC) and a means for flexibility is not provided, the RMC shall have a length of NOT more than _____.

A. 12 inches
B. 18 inches
C. 24 inches
D. 30 inches

2. Circuit breakers are NOT rated to carry 100 percent of the continuous load continuously unless they have a rating of at LEAST _____.

A. 100 amperes
B. 200 amperes
C. 400 amperes
D. 600 amperes

3. Where power-limited fire alarm (PLFA) circuit conductors pass through a wall, the conductors shall be protected by a metal raceway or nonmetallic conduit up to a of at LEAST _____ above the floor, unless other means of protection is provided.

A. 8 feet
B. 6 feet
C. 7 feet
D. 10 feet

4. When a receptacle is supplied from a 30-ampere rated branch circuit, the receptacle is required to have an ampere rating of _____ .

A. 30 amperes
B. 15 or 20 amperes
C. 20 or 30 amperes
D. 30 or 40 amperes

5. Transformers with ventilation openings shall be installed so the ventilating openings are not blocked by walls or other obstructions. The required clearances shall be _____ .

A. of not less than 3 inches
B. of not less than 6 inches
C. clearly marked on the transformer
D. as specified on the approved plans

6. A 3-phase, 480 volt wye service provided for a 3-phase motor load with no neutral load requires _____ .

A. a grounded service conductor be run to and isolated from the service disconnecting means
B. a grounding electrode conductor connected to the service disconnecting means
C. a grounded service conductor be run to and bonded to the service disconnecting means
D. no additional grounding or bonding

7. With respect to messenger-supported service-drop conductors and open overhead wiring operating at 0 to 750 volts to ground, the MINIMUM vertical clearance that must be maintained from the base of a swimming pool diving board and the conductors is _____ .

A. 22½ feet
B. 19½ feet
C. 14½ feet
D. 10 feet

8. Determine the MINIMUM required size 75 deg. C rated conductors permitted to be used to supply a demand load of 200 amperes where provided with a 208Y/120 volt, 3-phase 4-wire, electrical system. Consider all four (4) conductors to be current-carrying and the ambient temperature is 120 deg. F.

A. 250 kcmil
B. 300 kcmil
C. 400 kcmil
D. 500 kcmil

9. A metal junction box to be installed will contain the following conductors:

three - size 6 AWG ungrounded conductors
three - size 6 AWG grounded conductors
one size 8 AWG grounding conductor
three - size 12 AWG ungrounded conductors
three - size 12 AWG grounded conductors
one - size 12 AWG grounding conductor

The junction box is required to have a volume of at LEAST _____.

A. 51.50 cubic inches
B. 53.75 cubic inches
C. 46.50 cubic inches
D. 56.50 cubic inches

10. In regard to permanently installed swimming pools, where necessary to employ flexible connections to a pool pump motor, _____ shall be permitted as the wiring method(s).

   I. UF cable
   liquidtight flexible metal conduit (LFMC)

A. I only
B. II only
C. neither I nor II
D. both I and II

11. For emergency systems, where internal combustion engines are used as the prime mover, an on-site fuel supply shall be provided with an on premises fuel supply sufficient for NOT less than _____ full-demand operation of the system.

A. 2 hours
B. 3 hours
C. 4 hours
D. 8 hours

12. In regard to commercial garages, lamps and lampholders for fixed lighting located over lanes through which vehicles are commonly driven, shall be located NOT less than _____ above the floor level, unless the luminaires are of the totally enclosed type.

A. 8 feet
B. 10 feet
C. 12 feet
D. 14½ feet

13. Determine the maximum permitted operational setting of an adjustable inverse time circuit breaker used for branch-circuit, short-circuit and ground-fault protection of a 10 hp, 208-volt, 3-phase, squirrel cage, Design B, continuous-duty motor. Assume the motor will start at this setting and exceptions are not applicable.

A. 30.8 amperes
B. 35.7 amperes
C. 77.0 amperes
D. 338.8 amperes

14. Where seven (7) bridge cranes at an industrial facility are supplied from a common conductor system, the demand factor to be applied to the conductor system for the multiple cranes is _____ .

A. 95 percent
B. 87 percent
C. 81 percent
D. 78 percent

15. A photovoltaic power source for a dwelling shall be permitted to be connected to the load side of the service disconnect source, provided the sum of the ampere ratings of overcurrent devices supplying power to a busbar or conductor does NOT exceed _____ of the busbar rating.

A. 130 percent
B. 120 percent
C. 110 percent
D. 100 percent

16. Unless specifically identified for a higher percentage of fill, the cross-sectional area of the conductors in a conduit seal shall NOT exceed _____ of the cross-sectional area of a rigid metal conduit of the same trade size.

A. 25 percent
B. 40 percent
C. 50 percent
D. 60 percent

17. What MINIMUM size copper ungrounded conductors are permitted for use as service-entrance conductors for a one-family dwelling with a 120/240 volt, single-phase, electrical system, where the main circuit breaker has a rating of 200 amperes, but the computed demand load is only 100 amperes?

A. 4 AWG
B. 4/0 AWG
C. 2/0 AWG
D. 3/0 AWG

18. Use of a single overcurrent protective device for two-wire direct current generators shall be permitted ONLY when the device is actuated by _____ .

A. the entire current generated
B. entire current in the shunt field
C. entire current generated other than the current in the shunt field
D. half of the entire current generated

19. Determine the MAXIMUM standard size inverse time circuit breaker permitted for branch-circuit, short-circuit, and ground-fault protection for a 50 hp, ac motor, when given the following related information.

   continuous-duty
   induction type
   3-phase, 480 volt
   Design L
   nameplate rating 62 amperes

   A. 175 amperes
   B. 200 amperes
   C. 250 amperes
   D. 300 amperes

20. In general, on the load side of the point of grounding of a separately derived system such as a transformer, a grounded conductor is NOT permitted to be connected to _____ .

   A. equipment grounding conductors
   B. normally noncurrent-carrying metal parts of equipment
   C. ground, the earth
   D. any of these

21. The life safety branch of the emergency system of a health care facility shall provide power to _____ .

   I. automatic doors used for building egress
   illumination of electrical equipment rooms

   A. I only
   B. II only
   C. both I and II
   D. neither I nor II

22. Intrinsically safe apparatus, associated apparatus, and other equipment shall be installed _____ .

   A. in accordance with the control drawings
   B. in the electrical equipment room
   C. on a backboard of at least 3/4 in. thick plywood
   D. in a dedicated enclosure

23. The grounded conductor of a 3-phase, 3-wire, delta service shall have an ampacity NOT less than _____ .

A. that of the grounding conductor
B. that of the ungrounded conductors
C. 80 percent of the ungrounded conductors
D. 125 percent of the grounding conductor

24. Where a 150 kVA service transformer has a 480Y/120 volt, 3-phase primary and a 208Y/120 volt, 3-phase secondary, the full-load ampere rating on the primary side of the transformer is _____ .

A. 180 amperes
B. 312 amperes
C. 542 amperes
D. 416 amperes

25. Direct-buried cables or conductors located in a trench below 2 inch thick concrete or equivalent shall have a MINIMUM cover requirement of _____ .

A. 6 inches
B. 12 inches
C. 18 inches
D. 24 inches

END OF EXAM #16

ELECTRICIANS PRACTICE EXAMS
SIGN ELECTRICIAN
EXAM #17

The following questions are based on the 2011 edition of the National Electrical Code® and are typical of questions encountered on most Journeyman and Master Sign Electricians' Licensing Exams. Select the best answer from the choices given and review your answers with the answer key included in this book.

ALLOTTED TIME: 75 minutes

1. Which of the following conductor insulation types listed is NOT suitable for use in conduit buried underground in direct contact with the earth?

A. TW
B. THHN
C. THWN
D. XHHW

2. As long as it has continuity to the grounding electrode system, an equipment grounding conductor may be:

A. steel conduit.
B. the building steel structure member.
C. the building metallic water system.
D. All of these.

3. The MINIMUM length of free conductor to be left at each junction box for the purpose of splicing conductors, or making connections to luminaires or devices shall be _____ .

A. 4 inches
B. 6 inches
C. 8 inches
D. 10 inches

4. Where a 20-ampere, 120-volt, single-phase branch-circuit supplies an electric sign, what is the MAXIMUM voltage-drop the NEC® recommends on this branch-circuit?

A. 2.4 volts
B. 3.6 volts
C. 5.0 volts
D. 6.0 volts

5. Which of the following, if any, may be done to reduce voltage-drop on a branch-circuit?

   I. Install the conductors in a larger raceway.
   Increase the size of the ungrounded conductors.

A. I only
B. II only
C. either I or II
D. neither I nor II

6. When installing neon secondary circuit conductors over 1000 volts, metal parts of a building shall be permitted as _____.

A. a secondary return conductor
B. an equipment grounding conductor
C. a grounded conductor
D. none of these

7. Where installing rigid metal conduit (RMC) underground below a parking lot to supply an electric sign, what is the MINIMUM permitted burial depth of the conduit?

A. 6 inches
B. 12 inches
C. 18 inches
D. 24 inches

8. The National Electrical Code® requires equipment grounding conductors to be:

I. green in color or bare.
white or gray in color.

A. I only
B. II only
C. either I or II
D. neither I nor II

9. The required operating current for a specific luminous tube is dependent on which of the following?

A. junction box length
B. diameter of tubing
C. distance from adjacent tubing
D. branch circuit size

10. What is the MINIMUM size conductor permitted for wiring neon secondary circuits rated at 1000 volts or less?

A. 14 AWG
B. 12 AWG
C. 16 AWG
D. 18 AWG

11. The MAXIMUM number of size 8 AWG conductors with XHHW insulation permitted to be installed in a trade size 3/4 in. Schedule 40 PVC conduit, greater than 24 inches in length is _____ .

A. three
B. four
C. five
D. six

12. The NEC® requires a conductor that is properly identified with a solid yellow colored insulation to be a _____ conductor.

A. grounded
B. equipment grounding
C. ungrounded
D. bonded

13. With the exception of field-installed skeleton tubing (neon) all electric signs shall be _____ .

A. listed
B. labeled
C. provided with a 125-volt receptacle
D. provided with GFCI protection

14. Where an electric sign is installed in the parking lot of a retail shopping center and is not protected from physical damage, the sign is required to be at LEAST _____ above areas accessible to vehicles.

A. 10 feet
B. 12 feet
C. 14 feet
D. 16 feet

15. Branch-circuits that supply signs or outline lighting systems shall be rated NOT to exceed _____ .

A. 15 amperes
B. 20 amperes
C. 30 amperes
D. 50 amperes

16. Which one of the following listed types of connectors are prohibited for connection of an equipment grounding conductor to electric signs or their disconnecting means?

A. sheet metal screws
B. pressure connectors
C. clamps
D. lugs

17. An autotransformer which is used to raise the voltage to more than 300 volts, as part of a ballast for supplying lighting units, shall be supplied by a/an _____ system.

   I. grounded
   ungrounded

A. I only
B. II only
C. either I or II
D. neither I nor II

18. Branch circuit conductors installed in a ballast compartment located within three (3) inches of a ballast, shall have a temperature rating of NOT less than _____ .

A. 105 deg. C
B. 90 deg. C
C. 75 deg. C
D. 60 deg. C

19. Where installed in raceways, conductors LARGER than size _____ are required to be stranded.

A. 10 AWG
B. 8 AWG
C. 12 AWG
D. 14 AWG

20. Switches or similar devices controlling a transformer in a sign must have an ampere rating of NOT less than _____ of the ampere rating of the transformer.

A. 100 percent
B. 200 percent
C. 125 percent
D. 300 percent

21. Branch-circuit conductors supplying an electric sign load are required to have an ampacity of at LEAST _____ of the full-load current rating of the sign.

A. 100 percent
B. 115 percent
C. 150 percent
D. 125 percent

22. The spacing between wood or other combustible material and an incandescent or HID lamp or lampholder contained within an electric sign shall NOT be less than _____.

A. 1½ inches
B. 2 inches
C. 2½ inches
D. 3 inches

23. The MAXIMUM allowable ampacity of size 8 AWG THWN copper conductors installed in a 50 foot length of conduit is _____, when there are not more than three (3) current-carrying conductors in the conduit.

A. 40 amperes
B. 50 amperes
C. 55 amperes
D. 60 amperes

24. Each commercial building accessible to pedestrians shall have an outside sign circuit rated at LEAST _____ that supplies no other load.

A. 15 amperes
B. 20 amperes
C. 25 amperes
D. 30 amperes

25. What is the MAXIMUM distance permitted by the NEC® that a required disconnect may be located from an electric sign, unless the disconnecting means is capable of being locked in the open position?

A. 10 feet
B. 12 feet
C. 25 feet
D. 50 feet

END OF EXAM #17

ELECTRICIANS PRACTICE EXAMS
SIGN ELECTRICIAN
EXAM #18

The following questions are based on the 2011 edition the National Electrical Code® and are typical of questions encountered on most Journeyman and Master of Sign Electricians' Licensing Exams. Select the best answer from the choices given and review your answers with the answer key included in this book.

ALLOTTED TIME: 75 minutes

1. Where you have installed a transformer in an attic of a department store to supply an exterior electric sign, this installation is in compliance with the NEC® if there is an access door provided of at LEAST _____ .

A. 24 in. x 22½ in.
B. 36 in. x 22½ in.
C. 36 in. x 30 in.
D. 48 in. x 32 in.

2. Portable or mobile electric signs in damp or wet locations shall be provided with factory installed _____.

A. GLDI protection
B. AFCI protection
C. LCDI protection
D. GFCI protection

3. What is the MINIMUM number of 125-volt, single-phase, 15- or 20- ampere receptacle outlets the NEC® mandates to be installed in or on an electric sign?

A. None required
B. one
C. two
D. three

4. A portable or mobile electric sign shall not be placed WITHIN _____ horizontally from the inside walls of a decorative fountain.

A. 5 feet
B. 6 feet
C. 8 feet
D. 10 feet

5. When an electric sign is installed within a decorative fountain or within at LEAST _____ of the fountain edge, all branch circuits supplying the sign shall have GFCI protection provided for personnel.

A. 6 feet
B. 10 feet
C. 20 feet
D. 50 feet

6. The maximum ampere rating of an overcurrent device such as a circuit breaker or fuse protecting a branch-circuit, is directly dependent upon_____.

A. voltage
B. impedance
C. current flow
D. switch size

7. Determine the MINIMUM standard size listed metal box permitted by the NEC® that will contain two (2) size 12 AWG and three (3) size 8 AWG conductors.

A. 1 in. x 1¼ in. round
B. 3 in. x 2 in. x 1½ in. device
C. 4 in. x 1½ in. octagon
D. 3 in. x 2 in. x 2½ in. device

8. What is the MAXIMUM length allowed for cords supplying portable electric signs placed in dry locations?

A. 10 feet
B. 6 feet
C. 15 feet
D. 25 feet

9. The overcurrent protection for size 10 AWG copper conductors regardless of the temperature rating of the insulation, shall NOT exceed _____ , when protecting non-motorized electric sign loads.

A. 15 amperes
B. 20 amperes
C. 25 amperes
D. 30 amperes

10. Bonding conductors provided for electric signs shall be sized at NOT less than size _____ copper conductors.

A. 14 AWG
B. 12 AWG
C. 10 AWG
D. 8 AWG

11. Where installing a roof mounted metal electric sign enclosure made of sheet metal, the metal is required to be a MINIMUM thickness of _____ .

A. 0.202 in.
B. 0.020 in.
C. 0.160 in.
D. 0.016 in.

12. Flexible metal conduit (FMC) shall be permitted to be used outdoors, in wet locations, to enclose electric sign supply conductors _____ .

A. where the conductors are approved for use in wet locations
B. where the voltage to ground is not in excess of 120 volts
C. where the voltage to ground is not in excess of 300 volts
D. never

13. Rigid Schedule 40 PVC conduit, shall be securely fastened within at LEAST ____ of an outlet box, junction box, panelboard, or time clock.

A. 3 feet
B. 2½ feet
C. 2 feet
D. 1 foot

14. What is the MAXIMUM number of 90 degree bends permitted in a run of rigid Schedule 40 PVC conduit used to supply an electric sign if there are no junction boxes provided?

A. two
B. three
C. four
D. six

15. Where a commercial building having access to pedestrians has a branch-circuit supplying a sign containing neon tubing installations only, this branch-circuit shall be rated at a MAXIMUM of _____ .

A. 15 amperes
B. 20 amperes
C. 30 amperes
D. 40 amperes

16. The NEC® requires locations of lamps for outdoor lighting to be below all energized conductors or other electric utilization equipment; an exception to this requirement would be which of the following?

A. The lamps shall be within 6½ ft. of the ground level.
B. A lockable disconnecting means must be provided.
C. Conductors are to be identified by orange insulation.
D. The lamps must have a isolated grounding conductor.

17. Disregarding exceptions, when sign enclosures are supported by metal poles and the poles contain supply conductors to the sign, a handhole NOT less than _____ is required at the base of the pole to provide access to the supply terminations.

A. 2 in. x 4 in.
B. 4 in. x 4 in.
C. 4 in. x 6 in.
D. 6 in. x 6 in.

18. Which of the following is required, if any, for open branch circuit conductors that extend through the exterior wall of a building?

   I. The conductors must be in a metallic sleeve.

   Sleeves through the wall must slant upward from outside the building to inside the building.

A. I only
B. II only
C. both I and II
D. neither I nor II

19. What change in length, due to expansion, is a 200 foot run of Schedule 40 PVC conduit to have, where the PVC conduit is installed outdoors and is exposed to an annual 90 deg. F temperature variation from the warmest day to the coldest day?

A. 3.65 inches
B. 7.3 inches
C. 10.96 inches
D. 3.75 inches

20. For field-installed neon secondary conductors over 1000 volts, the length of the secondary circuit conductors from the transformer leads to the first neon tubing electrode shall NOT exceed _____ where installed in metal conduit or tubing.

A. 10 feet
B. 20 feet
C. 50 feet
D. 100 feet

21. When installing a service for a highway billboard electric sign consisting of three (3) 2-wire branch circuits only, the service disconnecting means shall have a rating of at LEAST _____ .

A. 15 amperes
B. 30 amperes
C. 60 amperes
D. 100 amperes

22. An electrical time clock for lighting is usually connected in _____ with a single lighting branch circuit to be controlled.

A. series
B. parallel
C. sequence
D. tandem

23. An electrical device used to reduce voltage without changing the available power is a/an _____.

A. rectifier
B. amplifier
C. transformer
D. capacitor

24. What is the MINIMUM size copper conductors required for an overhead span when serving a pole-mounted electric sign having a total load of 1,800 VA, when given the following conditions?

120 volt source
25 feet between supports
no messenger wire is provided

A. 8 AWG
B. 10 AWG
C. 12 AWG
D. 14 AWG

25. Given: A pole-mounted electric sign is to be installed at a convenience store having gasoline and diesel motor fuel dispensing units. The sign is to be supplied by conductors ran underground installed in a Schedule 40 PVC conduit. In order for the PVC to be outside the area classified as a hazardous location, the conduit is required to be at LEAST _____ from the motor fuel dispensing units.

A. 20 feet
B. 25 feet
C. 30 feet
D. 50 feet

END OF EXAM #18

Final Exams

ELECTRICIANS PRACTICE EXAMS
RESIDENTIAL ELECTRICIANS
FINAL EXAM

The following questions are based on the 2011 edition of the National Electrical Code® and are typical of questions encountered on most Residential Electricians' Licensing exams. Select the best answer from the choices given and review your answers with the answer key included in this book. Passing score on this exam is 70%. The exam consists of 75 questions valued at 1.33 points each; so you must answer at least 53 questions correct for a passing score. If you do not score at least 70%, try again and keep studying. GOOD LUCK.

ALLOTTED TIME: 4 hours

1. Where a mobile home has the main service disconnecting means installed outdoors, the disconnecting means shall be installed so the bottom of the enclosure is NOT less than _____ above finished grade.

A. one (1) foot
B. two (2) feet
C. three (3) feet
D. four (4) feet

2. Where nonmetallic-sheathed cable (NM) is installed in nonmetallic device boxes, the cable sheath shall not extend less than _____ inside the box and beyond any cable clamp.

A. 3/8 inch
B. 3/4 inch
C. 1/2 inch
D. 1/4 inch

3. Determine the MAXIMUM size circuit breaker that may be used to protect a 30 gallon residential water heater where given the following related information.

   water heater is rated 3,600 watts @ 240 volts
   conductors supplying the water heater are size 8 AWG

A. 15 amperes
B. 20 amperes
C. 25 amperes
D. 30 amperes

4. Determine the MINIMUM size copper nonmetallic sheathed cable (NM) permitted for use as branch-circuit conductors to supply a 17 kW, 240-volt, single-phase, household electric range.

A. 8 AWG
B. 6 AWG
C. 4 AWG
D. 2 AWG

5. Mobile home service equipment shall be rated NOT less than _____ for each mobile home it serves.

A. 100 amperes
B. 60 amperes
C. 125 amperes
D. 150 amperes

6. When nails are used to fasten metal boxes to wooden studs and the nails pass through the interior of the box, the nails shall be WITHIN _____ of the back of the box.

A. 1/4 in.
B. 1/2 in.
C. 3/8 in.
D. 3/4 in.

7. The largest size copper conductor permitted for nonmetallic sheathed cable (NM) is _____ .

A. 4 AWG
B. 1 AWG
C. 2/0 AWG
D. 2 AWG

8. For the purpose of determining conductor fill in a device box, the NEC® mandates a switch to be counted as equal to two (2) conductors. The volume allowance for the two (2) conductors shall be based on the _____ .

A. largest wire in the box
B. largest grounding conductor in the box
C. largest wire connected to the switch
D. number of clamps in the box

9. Where a 125-volt, single-phase, 20-ampere rated receptacle is provided for a washing machine in the laundry room of a dwelling, the receptacle shall be _____.

   I. listed tamper-resistant
   provided with GFCI protection

   A. I only
   B. II only
   C. both I and II
   D. neither I nor II

10. The ampacity of Type NM cable shall be in accordance with the _____ conductor temperature rating.

   A. 60 deg. C
   B. 75 deg. C
   C. 90 deg. C
   D. 90 deg. F

11. For residential electric ranges rated at 8.75 KW or more, the MINIMUM branch circuit rating shall be _____.

   A. 30 amperes
   B. 40 amperes
   C. 50 amperes
   D. 60 amperes

12. An outdoor receptacle provided for temporary Christmas decoration lighting placed in the soffit of a dwelling unit must be _____.

   A. a single receptacle
   B. located at least 6 ft., 6 in. above grade level
   C. GFCI protected
   D. removed after 90 days

13. Switching devices must be located at LEAST _____ from the inside walls of a permanently installed swimming pool, unless separated from the pool by a solid fence, wall, or other permanent barrier.

   A. 5 feet
   B. 10 feet
   C. 15 feet
   D. 20 feet

The NEC® considers an electric water heater to be _____.

   I. utilization equipment
   an appliance

A. I only
B. II only
C. neither I nor II
D. both I and II

15. The NEC® mandates the MAXIMUM length permitted for a flexible cord supplying a 120-volt, single-phase, room air-conditioner to be _____.

A. 4 feet
B. 6 feet
C. 8 feet
D. 10 feet

16. One-family dwellings with direct outdoor grade level access in front and back, are required to have _____.

   I. one receptacle outlet at the back
   one receptacle outlet at the front

A. I only
B. II only
C. both I and II
D. neither I nor II

17. Underground service conductors that are not encased in concrete and buried 18 inches or more below grade shall have their location identified by a warning ribbon that is placed in the trench at LEAST _____ above the underground installation.

A. 6 inches
B. 12 inches
C. 18 inches
D. 24 inches

18. When the white colored insulated conductor in a NM cable is used for a three-way switch loop, the conductor shall be _____.

A. permanently reidentified as an ungrounded conductor
B. a return conductor
C. used only for switch-leg conductors
D. a grounding conductor only

19. A premises wiring system supplied by a grounded ac service shall have a grounding electrode conductor connected to the _____ .

A. grounded service conductor
B. service disconnect enclosure
C. equipment grounding conductor
D. meter socket enclosure

20. Disregarding exceptions, fixed electric space heating loads of dwellings, shall be computed at what percent of the total computed load?

A. 100 percent
B. 110 percent
C. 115 percent
D. 80 percent

21. All 125-volt, single-phase receptacle outlets installed on a temporary service pole at a construction site are required to be _____ .

A. of the non-grounding type
B. of the grounding type and be provided with GFCI protection
C. rated 20 amperes
D. of the twist-lock type and rated at least 20 amperes

22. In dwellings, lighting outlets shall be permitted to be controlled by occupancy sensors provided they are _____.

A. automatic
B. located in the hallway
C. within six (6) feet of the door(s)
D. equipped with a manual override

23. Outdoor receptacles at a dwelling unit are NOT required to be GFCI protected if they are supplied from a dedicated branch circuit installed _____.

A. in a weatherproof box
B. at the second floor level
C. at least 6½ feet above grade level
D. for electric snow-melting or deicing equipment and not readily accessible

24. Where nonmetallic sheathed cable is used with nonmetallic boxes no larger than 2¼ in. x 4 in., the cable is not required to be secured to the box if the cable is fastened within at LEAST _____ of the box.

A. 6 inches
B. 8 inches
C. 12 inches
D. 10 inches

25. The smallest size aluminum conductors permitted for use as 120/240 volt, 3-wire, single-phase service-entrance conductors for a one-family dwelling is size _____ .

A. 8 AWG
B. 6 AWG
C. 4 AWG
D. 2 AWG

26. Insulated conductors shall be rated at _____ in type NM cable.

A. 60 deg. C
B. 75 deg. C
C. 90 deg. C
D. 90 deg. F

27. Where a direct-buried landscape lighting circuit that carries 24 volts is installed and type UF cable is the wiring method used, the cable must be buried with an earth cover of at LEAST _____ .

A. 6 inches
B. 12 inches
C. 18 inches
D. 24 inches

28. The power supply cord to a mobile home must NOT be longer than _____.

A. 21 feet
B. 26½ feet
C. 36½ feet
D. 50 feet

29. When trade size 3/8 in. flexible metal conduit (FMC) is used as a fixture whip from an outlet box to a luminaire, the flex shall NOT exceed _____ in length.

A. 10 feet
B. 4 feet
C. 5 feet
D. 6 feet

30. A cord-and-attachment plug connected room air-conditioner shall NOT exceed _____ of the rating of the branch circuit where no other loads are supplied.

A. 80 percent
B. 75 percent
C. 60 percent
D. 50 percent

31. Track lighting or ceiling fans are not to be located within a MINIMUM of _____ vertically from the top of the bathtub rim or shower stall threshold.

A. 6 feet
B. 8 feet
C. 4 feet
D. 2 feet

32. When Type NM cable is installed through slots or holes in metal framing members, the NEC® requires which of the following for the protection of the cable?

A. Listed bushings or grommets installed after cable installation.
B. Listed bushings or grommets installed before cable installation.
C. Split bushings or grommets installed after cable installation.
D. The NEC® permits any of these installations.

33. Low voltage landscape lighting systems operating at 30 volts or less shall be installed NOT less than _____ horizontally from the nearest edge of the water of a permanently installed swimming pool.

A. 6 feet
B. 8 feet
C. 10 feet
D. 15 feet

34. Disregarding exceptions, which of the following listed grounding electrodes must be supplemented by an additional electrode?

A. A metal underground water pipe.
B. A driven 8 ft. long ground rod.
C. A buried plate electrode.
D. All of these.

35. Which of the following listed overcurrent protection devices is NOT a standard ampere rating?

A. 50 amperes
B. 75 amperes
C. 90 amperes
D. 110 amperes

36. When driving a ground rod at a 45 degree angle and rock bottom is encountered, the electrode shall be permitted to be buried in a trench that is at LEAST _____ deep.

A. 36 inches
B. 30 inches
C. 48 inches
D. 24 inches

37. What is the MAXIMUM distance a 125-volt, single-phase, 15-or 20 ampere receptacle may be installed from a hot tub installed outdoors at a dwelling unit?

A. 20 feet
B. 15 feet
C. 10 feet
D. 5 feet

38. Where a dwelling unit has a utility room that houses heating, air-conditioning or refrigeration equipment requiring servicing, which of the following, if any, is/are mandated to be installed in the room?

   I. A 125-volt, single-phase, 15- or 20-ampere rated receptacle outlet.
   A switch controlled lighting outlet.

A. I only
B. II only
C. both I and II
D. neither I nor II

39. What is the MINIMUM number of 120-volt, 20-ampere rated branch circuits required for a one-family dwelling unit?

A. four
B. two
C. five
D. three

40. Using the standard method of calculation for a one-family dwelling, determine the MINIMUM demand load, in VA, on the ungrounded service-entrance conductors when the house has the following fixed appliances:

   water heater - 4,800 VA
   dishwasher - 1,200 VA
   garbage disposal - 1,150 VA
   trash compactor - 800 VA
   attic fan - 1,200 VA

A. 6,863 VA
B. 9,150 VA
C. 8,579 VA
D. 11,438 VA

41. In general, for size 10 AWG copper type NM cable the overcurrent protection shall NOTexceed _____ .

A. 25 amperes
B. 20 amperes
C. 35 amperes
D. 30 amperes

42. When a one-family dwelling having a demand load of 175 amperes is provided with a 120/240 volt, 3-wire, single-phase service-drop from the local utility company, what is the MINIMUM size THWN aluminum conductors permitted for use as ungrounded service-entrance conductors for the house?

A. 1/0 AWG
B. 2/0 AWG
C. 3/0 AWG
D. 4/0 AWG

43. When a 20-ampere rated branch circuit in a residence supplies only fixed resistance type baseboard heaters, this circuit may be loaded to a MAXIMUM value of _____ .

A. 16 amperes
B. 20 amperes
C. 18 amperes
D. 14 amperes

44. If an evaporative cooler or an air-conditioner is mounted on the roof of a multifamily dwelling, where is the service receptacle for the equipment to be located?

A. Within 75 feet of the unit.
B. Within 50 feet of the unit and on the same level.
C. Within 25 feet of the unit and on the same level.
D. Not required for dwelling units.

45. What is the MINIMUM size copper equipment grounding conductor required for a 15-ampere rated branch circuit installed in rigid metal conduit (RMC) that supplies a swimming pool pump motor?

A. 14 AWG
B. 12 AWG
C. 10 AWG
D. 8 AWG

46. For a one-family dwelling, at least one receptacle outlet shall be installed in each detached garage if the garage is:

A. more than 750 square feet in size.
B. less than 20 feet from the dwelling.
C. more than 20 feet from the dwelling.
D. provided with electric power.

47. The service grounding electrode conductor is sized by the rating of the_____.

A. main circuit breaker
B. service-drop conductors
C. service-entrance conductors
D. ground rod

48. When building a service for a residence, the grounded service entrance conductor shall NOT be smaller than the required _____.

A. grounding electrode conductor
B. largest phase conductor
C. ungrounded service-entrance conductor
D. largest feeder conductor

49. When wall-mounted, the required 125-volt, 15- and 20-ampere rated general-purpose receptacles in dwelling units, shall NOT be located more than _____ above the floor.

A. 5½ feet
B. 4 feet
C. 18 inches
D. 4½ feet

50. When a dwelling unit has a hallway 24 feet in length, the NEC® requires at LEAST _____ receptacle outlet(s) to be installed in the hallway.

A. one
B. two
C. three
D. four

51. In compliance with the NEC® where a 120-volt, 20-ampere branch circuit supplies multiple 15-ampere, duplex receptacles, the MAXIMUM cord-and-plug connected load, in amperes, any one receptacle is permitted to carry is _____ .

A. 15 amperes
B. 10 amperes
C. 8 amperes
D. 12 amperes

The service equipment for a mobile home is _____.

    I. permitted to be located on the exterior wall of the mobile home it serves

    II. required to be not more than 30 feet from the exterior wall of the mobile home it serves

A. I only
B. II only
C. both I and II
D. neither I nor II

53. In dwelling units, where 125-volt, 15- or 20-ampere receptacles are located MORE than_____ above the floor they shall not be required to be tamper-resistant.

A. 5 feet
B. 6 feet
C. 5½ feet
D. 6½ feet

54. Thermal insulation is not permitted to be installed above a recessed luminaire or WITHIN _____ of the recessed **luminaire's enclosure, wiring** compartment, ballast, transformer, LED driver, or power supply unless the luminaire is identified as Type IC for insulation contact.

A. 3 inches
B. 4 inches
C. 6 inches
D. 8 inches

55. A concrete-encased grounding electrode shall be permitted to consist of 20 feet of bare copper conductor NOT smaller than _____.

A. 1 AWG
B. 2 AWG
C. 3 AWG
D. 4 AWG

56. Foyers of dwelling units that are not part of a hallway that have an area that is GREATER than _____ shall have a receptacle(s) located in each wall space 3 feet or more in width and unbroken by doorways and similar openings.

A. 20 sq. ft.
B. 40 sq. ft.
C. 60 sq. ft.
D. 100 sq. ft.

57. In the NEC® conductor sizes are expressed in American Wire Gauge (AWG) or in _____ .

A. International Standard Gauge
B. circular centimeters
C. circular diameter
D. circular mils

58. Where exposed Type NM cable passes through a floor, the cable shall be protected from physical damage by an approved means extending at LEAST _____ above the floor.

A. 4 inches
B. 6 inches
C. 8 inches
D. 10 inches

59. Electrical equipment shall be installed in a _____ manner.

A. neat and workmanlike
B. neat and precise
C. secure and workmanlike
D. safe and secure

60. All 15- and 20-ampere, 125-volt and 250-volt nonlocking-type receptacles located outdoors in a wet location shall be listed _____ type.

A. weatherproof
B. raintight
C. weather-resistant
D. watertight

61. Where photovoltaic source and output circuits operating at maximum system voltages GREATER than _____ are installed in readily accessible locations, circuit conductors shall be installed in a raceway.

A. 12 volts
B. 24 volts
C. 30 volts
D. 50 volts

62. In dwelling units, cabinets or loadcenters containing overcurrent protection devices shall NOT be located in _____.

A. bedrooms
B. kitchens
C. hallways
D. bathrooms

63. Drywall or plasterboard surfaces that are damaged around boxes having a flush-type cover or faceplate shall be repaired so there will be no gaps greater than _____ at the edge of the box.

A. 1/8 in.
B. 1/4 in.
C. 3/8 in.
D. 1/2 in.

64. For dwelling units, all 15- and 20-ampere, single-phase, 125-volt receptacles located within at LEAST _____ or less of the inside walls of a permanently installed swimming pool shall be protected by a ground-fault circuit interrupter.

A. 5 feet
B. 6 feet
C. 10 feet
D. 20 feet

65. Where a dwelling unit is provided with a 120/240-volt, 3-wire, single-phase electrical system and has a demand load of 8 kVA and a total of six (6) branch circuits, the service disconnecting means shall have a rating of NOT less than _____ .

A. 40 amperes
B. 60 amperes
C. 100 amperes
D. 125 amperes

66. What is the MINIMUM number of general-use receptacle outlets required to be located in a residential kitchen island countertop with a long dimension of 48 inches and 18 inches wide?

A. none
B. one
C. two
D. three

67. Where a dwelling unit is provided with a deck or porch that is accessible from inside the dwelling, at least one 125-volt, 15- or 20-ampere receptacle outlet is required to be located within the perimeter of the deck or porch.

The receptacle shall NOT be located more than _____ above the deck or porch surface.

A. 2 feet
B. 4 feet
C. 5 feet
D. 6½ feet

68. Where a size 8 AWG Type NM cable is used to supply a 5,000 watt, 240 volt, single-phase residential cooktop, the MAXIMUM standard size circuit breaker permitted for overcurrent protection for this appliance has a rating of _____ .

A. 35 amperes
B. 30 amperes
C. 25 amperes
D. 40 amperes

69. Conductors tapped from a 50-ampere branch circuit supplying household cooking appliances such as, electric ranges, ovens and cooktops shall have an ampacity of NOT less than _____ and shall be of sufficient size for the load to be served.

A. 30 amperes
B. 20 amperes
C. 40 amperes
D. 45 amperes

70. In dwelling unit bathrooms, where a receptacle outlet is located on the side or face of the basin cabinet, the outlet shall NOT be more than _____ below the countertop.

A. 8 inches
B. 10 inches
C. 12 inches
D. 18 inches

71. When the white-colored insulated conductor in a Type NM cable is used for a three-way switch loop, the conductor shall be reidentified and used only_____.

A. as a grounding conductor
B. as a return conductor
C. for a traveler
D. as an ungrounded conductor to supply the switch

72. General-use receptacle outlets placed in floors of dwelling units shall not be counted as part of the required number of receptacle outlets unless located WITHIN _____ of the wall.

A. 18 inches
B. 20 inches
C. 22 inches
D. 24 inches

73. In general, where a cable or raceway is installed through bored holes in wood members, holes shall be bored so that the edge of the hole is NOT less than _____ from the nearest edge of the wood member.

A. 1 in.
B. 1¼ in.
C. 1½ in.
D. ¾ in.

74. Given: Type UF cable is to be used for direct buried residential branch circuits of 120-volts to supply area lighting. The conductors will be GFCI protected with an overcurrent protection of 20 amperes; the cables will not cross under any driveways or concrete. What is the MINIMUM permitted burial depth of the cable?

A. 6 inches
B. 12 inches
C. 18 inches
D. 24 inches

75. For low-voltage landscape lighting systems operating at 30 volts or less, the output circuits of the power supply are to be rated for NOT more than _____.

A. 15 amperes
B. 20 amperes
C. 25 amperes
D. 30 amperes

END OF RESIDENTIAL ELECTRICIANS FINAL EXAM

NOTES

ELECTRICIANS PRACTICE EXAMS
JOURNEYMAN ELECTRICIAN
FINAL EXAM

The following questions are based on the 2011 edition of the National Electrical Code® and are typical of questions encountered on most Journeyman Electricians' Licensing Exams. Select the best answer from the choices given and review your answers with the answer key included in this book. Passing score on this exam IS 70%. The exam consists of 80 questions valued at 1.25 points each, therefore you must

answer 56 questions correct for a passing score. If you do not score at least 70%, try again and keep studying. GOOD LUCK.

ALLOTTED TIME: 4 hours

1. The MINIMUM height of service-drop conductors, where not in excess of 600 volts, installed over an apple orchard or orange grove is _____ above ground.

A. 12 feet
B. 15 feet
C. 21 feet
D. 18 feet

2. According to the NEC®, a conductor with three (3) white stripes on a black background is permitted to be used as a _____ conductor.

A. ungrounded
B. grounding
C. grounded
D. hot phase

3. Flexible metal tubing (FMT) is permitted to be used as a wiring method in _____ .

A. accessible locations
B. wet locations
C. damp locations
D. hoistways

4. The interior of an exhaust duct used to vent vapors from a paint booth is classified as a _____ hazardous location.

A. Class I, Division 1
B. Class I, Division 2
C. Class II, Division 1
D. Class II, Division 2

5. When wiring motor fuel dispensing pumps, the first fitting that should be installed in the raceway that emerges from below ground or concrete into the base of the gasoline dispenser is a/an:

A. automatic cut-off breakaway valve.
B. disconnect.
C. sealing fitting.
D. no fittings of any kind are permitted in this location.

6. One kVA is equal to _____.

A. one hundred watts
B. one thousand volt-amps
C. one hundred kilo-watts
D. one hundred volt-amps

7. A 15 kW, 208-volt, single-phase heat-pump has a full-load current rating of _____.

A. 42 amperes
B. 125 amperes
C. 65 amperes
D. 72 amperes

8. Heavy-duty lighting track is lighting track identified for use exceeding _____.

A. 15 amperes
B. 600 watts
C. 20 amperes
D. 120 volts

9. When installed, a metal junction box will contain the following conductors:

   three - 6 AWG wires, 2 ungrounded & 1 grounded
   one - 8 AWG equipment grounding conductor
   two - internal clamps
   one - pigtail

Determine the MINIMUM size box, in cubic inches, the NEC® requires.

A. 16 cubic inches
B. 18 cubic inches
C. 20 cubic inches
D. 23 cubic inches

10. Live parts of generators operated at MORE than _____ to ground shall not be exposed to accidental contact where accessible to unqualified persons.

A. 24 volts
B. 50 volts
C. 120 volts
D. 150 volts

11. In general, in patient care areas, the wiring of the emergency system in hospitals must be installed in _____ .

A. flexible metal raceways
B. nonflexible metal raceways
C. flexible nonmetallic raceways
D. nonflexible nonmetallic raceways

12. On land, the service equipment for floating structures and submersible electrical equipment shall be located NO closer than _____ horizontally from the shoreline.

A. 5 feet
B. 10 feet
C. 15 feet
D. 20 feet

13. Determine the MINIMUM size 75 deg. C rated copper conductors required to supply a fixed electric space heating unit with heating elements having a full-load current rating of 125 amperes and a blower motor having a full-load current rating of 2.5 amperes.

A. 1 AWG
B. 2 AWG
C. 2/0 AWG
D. 3/0 AWG

14. Where a thermal protector is integral with the motor, the ultimate trip current of a thermally protected 2 horsepower, single-phase, 240-volt motor shall NOT exceed _____ of the full-load current of the motor.

A. 115 percent
B. 125 percent
C. 140 percent
D. 156 percent

15. Under which one of the following conditions are you required to use an approved electrically conductive corrosion resistance compound on metal conduit threads?

A. In Class I Division 1 locations.
B. In Class II Division 1 locations.
C. On field cut threads for indoor locations.
D. On field cut threads in corrosive locations.

16. Disregarding exceptions, each patient bed location in critical care areas of hospitals shall be supplied by:

  I. one or more branch circuits from the emergency system.
  one or more branch circuits from the normal system.

A. I only
B. II only
C. either I or II
D. both I and II

Copyright© 2016

17. Freestanding-type, cord-and-plug connected office partitions, shall not contain more than _____ 15-ampere, 125-volt receptacles.

A. six
B. thirteen
C. ten
D. eight

18. In general, overhead service-drop conductors shall NOT be smaller than size _____.

A. 8 AWG copper
B. 6 AWG copper
C. 8 AWG aluminum
D. 2 AWG aluminum

19. What MINIMUM size bonding conductor must bond all metal parts associated with a hot tub?

A. 12 AWG
B. 10 AWG
C. 8 AWG
D. 6 AWG

20. When installing galvanized rigid metal conduit (RMC), where structural members readily permit fastening, the conduit is required to be fastened within at LEAST _____ of a junction box, panelboard or cabinet.

A. 3 feet
B. 5 feet
C. 6 feet
D. 10 feet

21. In general, the disconnecting means for motor circuits rated 600 volts or less, shall have an ampere rating of at LEAST what percent of the full-load current rating of the motor supplied?

A. 80 percent
B. 100 percent
C. 115 percent
D. 125 percent

22. Given: A 240-volt wye-connected motor derives power from a converted single-phase source. It is desired to connect a 120/240 volt transformer for control of the motor on the load side of the converter. The control transformer must _____ .

A. be connected to the manufactured phase
B. be disconnected after start-up of the motor
C. have separate overcurrent protection
D. not be connected to the manufactured phase

23. What is the MAXIMUM size overcurrent protection device required to protect size 14 AWG conductors used for the pump motor control-circuit that is protected by the motor branch circuit protection device and extends beyond the enclosure?

A. 15 amperes
B. 20 amperes
C. 45 amperes
D. 100 amperes

24. Where raceways are installed above grade outdoors and exposed to the weather, the interior of these raceways shall be considered to be a _____ location.

A. damp
B. moist
C. dry
D. wet

25. In general, a generator that does NOT require overcurrent protection is a _____ .

A. two-wire generator
B. constant voltage generator
C. generator operating at 65 volts or less
D. three-wire, direct current generator

26. A motor overload device functions in direct response to _____ .

A. voltage
B. motor current
C. temperature rise of the motor
D. ambient temperature

27. When a cord-and-plug connected water softener is wired to a 20 ampere rated branch-circuit, the SMALLEST size flexible cord to supply the water softener as permitted by the NEC® is size _____.

A. 18 AWG
B. 16 AWG
C. 14 AWG
D. 20 AWG

28. When twenty (20) size 10 AWG copper current-carrying conductors with THHN insulation are installed in a 50 feet run of trade size 1½ in. electrical metallic tubing (EMT), what is the allowable ampacity rating of each conductor?

A. 15 amperes
B. 20 amperes
C. 25 amperes
D. 30 amperes

29. Flexible metal conduit (FMC) is permitted for use in wet locations _____.

A. when the conductors within the FMC have a temperature rating of not less than 90 deg. C
B. when the conductors contained within the FMC are approved for use in wet locations
C. where the length of the FMC is not more than six (6) feet
D. under no circumstances

30. The MINIMUM size copper wire that may be used for grounding the secondary of an instrument transformer is _____.

A. 6 AWG
B. 8 AWG
C. 10 AWG
D. 12 AWG

31. In general, which one of the following statements is TRUE regarding the required disconnecting means for a fluorescent luminaire.

A. Only the ungrounded conductor to the ballast is required to be disconnected when connected to multiwire branch circuits.
B. The disconnecting means shall not be external to the luminaire.
C. The disconnecting means shall simultaneously break all supply conductors to the ballast, when connected to a multiwire branch circuit.
D. The disconnecting means shall be external to the luminaire.

32. Control-circuit conductors and motor branch-circuits are permitted by the NEC® to occupy the same raceway, if the control circuit conductors _____.

A. carry no more than 24 volts
B. have a voltage to ground not to exceed 150 volts
C. have a voltage to ground not to exceed 277 volts
D. are functionally associated with the motor system

33. A motor that is operation for alternate intervals of (1) load and no load, or (2) load and rest, or (3) load, no load and rest, is defined as being _____ duty.

A. periodic
B. intermittent
C. varying
D. short-time

34. A feeder supplying two (2) continuous-duty, 208-volt, 3-phase motors, one 10 hp and one 7½ hp shall have a MINIMUM ampacity of _____ amperes.

A. 55.00
B. 68.75
C. 62.70
D. 38.50

35. The reason the NEC® requires all phase conductors of the same circuit to be in the same ferrous metal raceway is to reduce _____ .

A. expense
B. inductive heat
C. voltage drop
D. resistance

36. Which of the following conductor insulation types, if any, is/are acceptable for wiring in a fluorescent luminaire when the branch circuit conductor passes within three (3) inches of the ballast?

   I. THW
   THWN

A. I only
B. II only
C. both I and II
D. neither I nor II

37. Where practicable, a separation of at LEAST _____ shall be maintained between communications wires and cables on buildings and lightning conductors.

A. 18 inches
B. 24 inches
C. 4 feet
D. 6 feet

38. A fluorescent luminaire shall be permitted to be cord connected _____ .

A. where the flexible cord is contained in an approved raceway
B. where the flexible cord is visible for its entire length
C. where the flexible cord is at least size 12 AWG
D. never

39. An attachment plug-and-receptacle may be permitted to serve as a motor controller if the motor is portable and has a MAXIMUM rating of _____.

A. 1/8 HP
B. 1/4 HP
C. 1/3 HP
D. 1/2 HP

40. An equipotential bonding grid must be installed in the deck around a permanently installed swimming pool; the bonding grid shall extend for at LEAST _____ horizontally beyond the inside walls of the pool.

A. 3 feet
B. 5 feet
C. 6 feet
D. 10 feet

41. A plumbing pipe passing 66 inches above a switchboard located indoors is _____ .

A. permitted if a drip pan is installed over the switchboard
B. not permitted
C. permitted above an accessible suspended ceiling
D. permitted when the switchboard is rated NEMA 3R

42. All spa and hot tub equipment installed in non-dwelling occupancies shall be provided with an emergency shutoff or control switch within sight of the unit(s), and located NOT less than _____ from the inside wall of the spa or hot tub.

A. 6 feet
B. 10 feet
C. 5 feet
D. 12 feet

43. Feeders to floating buildings are permitted to be installed in _____ where flexible connections are required.

A. MC cable
B. AC cable
C. NMC cable
D. portable power cable

44. In an open paint spraying area, the Class I, Division 2 area shall extend vertically above the Class I, Division 1 or Class I, Zone 1 area for at LEAST _____ .

A. 5 feet
B. 10 feet
C. 15 feet
D. 20 feet

45. In a marina, the disconnecting means for a boat receptacle must be readily accessible and NOT more than _____ from the receptacle.

A. 6 feet
B. 10 feet
C. 30 inches
D. 50 feet

46. Branch circuit conductors supplying a varying duty motor with a 30 minute and/or 60 minute rating shall have an ampacity of at LEAST _____ of the nameplate rating of the motor to be supplied.

A. 85 percent
B. 110 percent
C. 120 percent
D. 150 percent

47. Cablebus shall be installed only for _____ locations.

A. exposed
B. commercial
C. concealed
D. hazardous

48. Where solar photovoltaic systems have both ac and dc systems requiring grounding _____ .

A. the ac grounding electrodes must be isolated from the dc grounding electrodes
B. a common ground bus is not permitted to be used for both systems
C. the dc grounding system shall be bonded to the ac grounding system
D. both systems shall have a minimum size 2 AWG grounding electrode conductor

49. A hospital conference room is considered to be an assembly occupancy when designed for the assembly of at LEAST _____ or more persons.

A. 25
B. 50
C. 75
D. 100

50. Determine the MINIMUM required size 75 deg. C rated conductors to supply a demand load of 200 amperes where installed in an area with an expected ambient temperature of 120 deg. F.

A. 3/0 AWG
B. 4/0 AWG
C. 300 kcmil
D. 250 kcmil

51. Where concrete encased, raceways approved for burial only shall require a concrete envelope NOT less than _____ thick.

A. 2 inches
B. 4 inches
C. 6 inches
D. 8 inches

52. Overhead communications wires and cables shall have a separation of at LEAST ____ from supply service-drops of 0-750 volts at any point in the span.

A. 30 inches
B. 24 inches
C. 12 inches
D. 18 inches

53. In general, electrical nonmetallic tubing (ENT) shall be securely fastened in place within at LEAST _____ of each outlet box, junction box, or panelboard.

A. 12 inches
B. 18 inches
C. 24 inches
D. 36 inches

54. Where flexible cord has one conductor identified by a ridge on the exterior of the cord, this conductor is identified as a/an _____ conductor.

A. ungrounded
B. grounded
C. phase
D. equipment grounding

55. Where a raceway enters a building or structure from an underground distribution system, it shall be _____.

A. sealed
B. marked
C. Schedule 40 PVC only
D. provided with a drain hole

56. Equipment grounding conductors used for systems over 1 kV that are not an integral part of a cable assembly shall NOT be smaller than _____ copper.

A. 8 AWG
B. 6 AWG
C. 4 AWG
D. 2 AWG

57. What is the MAXIMUM number of size 4 AWG THHN copper conductors permitted to be installed in a trade size 1¼ in. electrical metallic tubing (EMT) having a length of 18 inches?

A. 10
B. 11
C. 12
D. 13

58. What is the MINIMUM size 75 deg. C copper ungrounded (phase) service entrance conductors permitted for a 200 ampere rated commercial service?

A. 4/0 THW
B. 2/0 THW
C. 3/0 THHN
D. 3/0 THW

59. Where a surfaced-mounted luminaire containing a ballast, transformer, LED driver, or power supply is to be installed on combustible low-density cellulose fiberboard, it shall be marked for this condition or shall be spaced NOT less than _____ from the surface of the fiberboard.

A. 3/4 in.
B. 1 in.
C. 1¼ in.
D. 1½ in.

60. Which of the following listed cables have an overall covering that is fungus resistant?

A. Type NM
B. Type NMS
C. Type NMC
D. Type MI

61. The conductors in multiconductor portable cables of over 600 volts, used to connect mobile equipment and machinery, shall be at LEAST size _____ copper or larger and employ flexible stranding.

A. 14 AWG
B. 12 AWG
C. 10 AWG
D. 8 AWG

62. Where a conductor is marked *RHW-2* on the insulation, what does the *-2* represent?

A. The cable has 2 conductors.
B. The cable is double insulated.
C. The conductor has a nylon outer jacket.
D. The conductor has a maximum operating temperature of 90°C.

63. Given: Conductors of not over 25 ft. long are to be tapped from a service where two (2) parallel size 500 kcmil copper conductors per phase are protected by an 800 ampere overcurrent protection device. The tap conductors will terminate in a single circuit breaker. What MINIMUM size THW copper conductors are required for the tap conductors?

A. 500 kcmil
B. 400 kcmil
C. 300 kcmil
D. 250 kcmil

64. Gas or oil central space heating equipment shall be _____.

A. supplied from an individual branch circuit
B. provided with GFCI protection
C. provided with LCDI protection
D. permitted to be supplied from a general-use branch circuit supplying other equipment

65. Given: A 12 unit condo will have an 8 kW electric range in each unit; apply the optional method of calculation for multifamily dwellings and calculate the demand load, in kW, on the ungrounded (line) service entrance conductors for the electric ranges.

A. 39.4 kW
B. 30.7 kW
C. 25.9 kW
D. 32.0 kW

66. A designated information technology equipment room is required to be _____ .

A. sound-proofed
B. provided with at least two exit doors
C. equipped with walls at least 6 inches thick
D. separated from other occupancies by fire-resistant-rated walls, floors and ceilings

67. The classification of hazardous areas and zones is to be determined by _____ .

A. engineers
B. licensed electricians
C. qualified persons
D. the local authority having jurisidiction

68. When installing border lighting for stages in theaters, the luminaires shall be arranged so that no branch circuit will carry a load to exceed _____ .

A. 10 amperes
B. 20 amperes
C. 15 amperes
D. 30 amperes

69. Where a single device wider than two (2) inches is installed in a 2-gang device box, the device is to be counted as equal to _____ conductor(s).

A. one
B. two
C. three
D. four

70. The allowable ampacity of size 22 AWG conductors of instrumentation tray cable shall be _____ .

A. 3 amperes
B. 5 amperes
C. 7 amperes
D. 10 amperes

71. Type AC cable shall be permitted _____ .

A. for feeders
B. in wet locations
C. in damp locations
D. where exposed to physical damage

72. Where the outer sheath of Type MI cable is made of steel _____ .

A. it shall provide an adequate path to serve as an equipment grounding conductor
B. a separate equipment grounding conductor shall be provided
C. the grounding and grounded conductors shall be connected together
D. it shall not be longer than 6 feet

73. Where electrical metallic tubing (EMT) is installed under metal-corrugated sheet roof decking, a clearance of at LEAST _____ must be maintained between the tubing and the surface of the roof decking.

A. 1 in.
B. 1¼ in.
C. 1½ in.
D. 2 in.

74. A neutral conductor is always _____ .

A. a grounded conductor not intended to carry current
B. an ungrounded conductor
C. white in color
D. the conductor connected to the neutral point of a system that is intended to carry current under normal conditions

75. Where an intermediate metal conduit (IMC) located 2 inches above a rooftop and exposed to direct sunlight contains three (3) current-carrying size 500 kcmil 75°C rated copper conductors, in an area where the expected ambient temperature is 86°F, the allowable ampacity of the conductors is _____ .

A. 380 amperes
B. 312 amperes
C. 255 amperes
D. 289 amperes

76. The insulated conductors of Type TC cables shall be in sizes _____ to 1000 kcmil copper, nickel, or nickel-coated copper.

A. 18 AWG
B. 16 AWG
C. 14 AWG
D. 12 AWG

77. In general, all panelboards are required to have overcurrent protection, an EXCEPTION to this rule is _____ .

A. panelboards containing less than 42 overcurrent devices
B. panelboards containing only single-pole overcurrent devices
C. panelboards that supply a second bus structure within the same panelboard
D. for existing panelboards used as service equipment in a one-family dwelling

78. Where a motor controller that is not an inverse time circuit breaker or molded case switch, controls a 120 hp, continuous-duty, ac motor of not over 600 volts, the controller shall have a horsepower rating of NOT less than _____ .

A. 120 hp
B. 150 hp
C. 175 hp
D. 200 hp

79. Overload relays and other devices for motor overload protection that are NOT capable of opening short-circuits or ground-faults shall be protected by a motor short-circuit protector or by _____.

A. an instantaneous trip circuit breaker only
B. fuses or circuit breakers
C. Class CC fuses only
D. a ground-fault circuit interrupter

80. An electrical system comprised of multiple power sources is known as a/an _____ .

A. emergency system
B. optional standby system
C. hybrid system
D. legally required standby system

END OF JOURNEYMAN ELECTRICIANS FINAL EXAM

ELECTRICIANS PRACTICE EXAMS
MASTER ELECTRICIAN
FINAL EXAM

The following questions are based on the 2011 edition of the National Electrical Code® and are typical of questions encountered on most Master Electricians' Licensing Exams. Select the best answer from the choices given and review your answers with the answer key included in this book. Passing score on this exam is 75%. The exam consists of 100 questions valued at 1.0 point each, so you must answer 75 questions correct for a passing score. If you do not score at least 75%, try again and keep studying. GOOD LUCK.

ALLOTTED TIME: 5 hours

1. Given: After all demand factors have been taken into consideration for an office building, the demand load is determined to be 90,000 VA; the building has a 120/240 volt, single-phase electrical system. What MINIMUM size copper conductors with THHN/THWN insulation are required for the ungrounded service-lateral conductors?

A. 400 kcmil
B. 350 kcmil
C. 300 kcmil
D. 500 kcmil

2. Given: A commercial building is to be supplied from a transformer having a 480Y/277 volt, 3-phase primary and a 208Y/120 volt, 3-phase secondary. The secondary will have a balanced computed demand load of 416 amperes per phase. The transformer is required to have a MINIMUM kVA rating of _____.

A. 100 kVA
B. 150 kVA
C. 86 kVA
D. 200 kVA

3. Manhole covers shall be OVER _____ or otherwise require the use of tools to open.

A. 25 lbs.
B. 50 lbs.
C. 75 lbs.
D. 100 lbs.

4. The branch circuit conductors supplying one or more units of information technology equipment shall have an ampacity of NOT less than _____ of the connected load.

A. 80 percent
B. 100 percent
C. 115 percent
D. 125 percent

5. In regard to a 7½ hp, 480-volt, 3-phase ac motor with an 80 percent power factor and a full-load ampere rating of 19 amperes indicated on the nameplate, and a service factor of 1.15; when the initial setting of the overload device you have selected is not sufficient to carry the load, what is the MAXIMUM setting permitted for the overload protection?

A. 21.85 amperes
B. 23.75 amperes
C. 24.70 amperes
D. 26.60 amperes

6. Health care facilities require ground fault protection:

A. on all 208Y/120 volt, 3-phase, 4-wire systems.
B. on the next level of feeders after the service disconnect.
C. to be omitted from all life-safety branch-circuits.
D. on all essential electrical systems feeders.

7. What MINIMUM voltage is required after 1½ hours to serve emergency lighting from a storage battery, when the normal source voltage of 120 volts is interrupted?

A. 60 volts
B. 90 volts
C. 105 volts
D. 120 volts

8. Determine the MAXIMUM ampere setting permitted for an overload protective device responsive to motor current, where used to protect a 20 hp, 240-volt, 3-phase, induction type ac motor with a temperature rise of 48 deg. C and a FLA of 54 amperes indicated on the nameplate.

A. 54.0 amperes
B. 70.2 amperes
C. 62.1 amperes
D. 75.6 amperes

9. Atmospheres containing combustible metal dust such as aluminum or magnesium are considered to be in material _____ classifications.

A. Group C
B. Group D
C. Group E
D. Group F

10. Aluminum or steel cable trays shall be permitted to be used as equipment grounding conductors, provided _____ .

    I. the cable tray sections and fittings are identified as an equipment grounding conductor
    II. the cable tray sections and fittings are durably marked to show the cross-sectional area of the metal

A. I only
B. II only
C. neither I nor II
D. both I and II

11. When intermediate metal conduit (IMC) is threaded in the field, a standard cutting die with a _____ taper per ft. shall be used.

A. 3/8 in.
B. 1/2 in.
C. 3/4 in.
D. 1 in.

12. In regard to emergency systems, where internal combustion engines are used as the prime movers, they shall NOT be solely dependent on a public utility gas system for their fuel supply, unless _____ .

A. it is acceptable to the authority having jurisdiction
B. the gas system is listed and approved
C. the gas system and electrical utility are jointly owned and maintained
D. none of these apply

13. When a motor controller enclosure is installed outdoors and is subject to be exposed to sleet, it shall have a MINIMUM rating of _____, where the controller mechanism is required to be operable when ice covered.

A. Type 3
B. Type 3S
C. Type 3R
D. Type 3SX

14. Nonmetallic underground conduit with conductors (NUCC) larger than trade size _____ shall not be used.

A. 2 in.
B. 3 in.
C. 4 in.
D. 6 in.

15. Ceiling-suspended luminaires (lighting fixtures) or paddle fans located _____ or more above the maximum water level of an indoor installed spa or hot tub shall NOT require GFCI protection.

A. 10 feet
B. 7½ feet
C. 8 feet
D. 12 feet

16. When flat conductor cable (FCC) is used for general-purpose branch circuits, the MAXIMUM rating of the circuits shall be _____ .

A. 20 amperes
B. 30 amperes
C. 15 amperes
D. 10 amperes

17. When sizing overcurrent protection for fire pump motors, the device(s) shall be selected or set to carry indefinitely the _____ of the motor.

A. starting current
B. full-load running current
C. locked-rotor current
D. full-load amperage as indicated on the nameplate

18. Under which, if any, of the following conditions is the neutral conductor to be counted as a current-carrying conductor?

　I. When it is only carrying the unbalanced current.
　When it is the neutral conductor of a 3-phase, wye-connected system that consist of nonlinear loads.

A. I only
B. II only
C. neither I nor II
D. both I and II

19. In general, all mechanical elements used to terminate a grounding electrode conductor or bonding jumper to a grounding electrode shall be accessible. Which of the following, if any, is/are an exception(s) to this rule?

　I. A connection to a concrete encased electrode.
　A compression connection to fire-proofed structural metal.

A. I only
B. II only
C. neither I nor II
D. both I and II

20. What type of luminaire must be used in a totally enclosed poultry house when condensation may be present?

A. explosion proof
B. nonmetallic
C. suitable for use in damp locations
D. suitable for use in wet locations

21. Fuses shall NOT be permitted to be connected in parallel where _____.

   I. they are factory assembled and listed as a unit
   they are installed by a technician on the jobsite

A. I only
B. II only
C. neither I nor II
D. both I and II

22. Each multiwire branch circuit shall be provided with a means that will _____ at the point where the branch circuit originates.

A. simultaneously disconnect all ungrounded conductors
B. not simultaneously disconnect all ungrounded conductors
C. simultaneously disconnect all grounded and ungrounded conductors
D. simultaneously disconnect all grounded, ungrounded and grounding conductors

23. When calculating the total load for a mobile home park before demand factors are taken into consideration, each individual mobile home lot shall be calculated at a MINIMMUM of _____.

A. 20,000 VA
B. 15,000 VA
C. 24,000 VA
D. 16,000 VA

24. A single electrode consisting of a ground rod, pipe, or plate that does not have a resistance to ground of 25 ohms or less, shall be supplemented by one (1) additional electrode. Which of the following listed is/are approved for this purpose?

A. a concrete-encased electrode
B. a ground ring
C. the metal frame of the building
D. all of these

25. What classified (hazardous) location(s), if any, does the NEC® permit flexible metal conduit (FMC) for connections to motors?

   I. Class I, Div. 2
   Class II, Div. 1

   A. I only
   B. II only
   C. both I and II
   D. Neither I nor II

26. At carnivals and fairs, service equipment shall not be installed in a location that is accessible to unqualified persons unless the equipment _____.

   A. is lockable
   B. is provided with GFCI protection
   C. is installed at a height of 6 feet or greater
   D. has a voltage to ground of not more than 125 volts

27. Nonmetallic surface extensions shall be permitted to be run in any direction from an existing outlet, but NOT within _____ of the floor level.

   A. 1 foot
   B. 1½ feet
   C. 2 feet
   D. 2 inches

28. The NEC® permits a building to have more than one service when:

   the load requirements of the building are at least in excess of 800 amperes.
   the building is separated by firewalls with a four-hour rating.

   A. I only
   B. II only
   C. either I or II
   D. neither I nor II

29. In the garage of a dwelling unit, a 125-volt, single-phase, 15 ampere, receptacle installed in the ceiling provided for the garage door opener must be _____ .

I. a single receptacle
GFCI protected for personnel

A. I only
B. II only
C. either I or II
D. neither I nor II

30. Which one of the following wiring methods is permitted to be installed in air ducts specifically fabricated for environmental air?

A. Schedule 40 PVC conduit
B. electrical metallic tubing (EMT)
C. armored cable (AC)
D. nonmetallic sheathed cable (NM)

31. Outlets supplying permanently installed swimming pool pump motors from single-phase, 15- or 20-ampere, 120 or 240 volt branch circuits, shall be provided with GFCI protection _____ .

A. where installed outdoors
B. when cord-and-plug connected
C. when direct (hard-wired) connected
D. where any of the above conditions exist

32. The branch circuit conductors supplying a 240-volt, single-phase, 15 kW rated fixed electric space heater provided with a 10 ampere blower motor are required to have an ampacity of at LEAST _____ .

A. 63 amperes
B. 78 amperes
C. 91 amperes
D. 109 amperes

33. A commercial kitchen is to contain the following listed cooking related equipment:

   one - 14 kW range
   one - 5.0 kW water heater
   one - 0.75 kW mixer
   one - 2.5 kW dishwasher
   one - 2.0 kW booster heater
   one - 2.0 kW broiler

Determine the demand load, in kW, after applying the demand factors for the kitchen equipment.

A. 19.00 kW
B. 26.25 kW
C. 18.38 kW
D. 17.06 kW

34. When two (2) ground rods are used to form the entire grounding electrode system of a building, the grounding conductor that bonds the two rods together shall NOT be required to be larger than size _____ copper, regardless of the size of the service-entrance conductors.

A. 8 AWG
B. 6 AWG
C. 4 AWG
D. 2 AWG

35. A kitchen with a total demand load of 54,000 VA is to be added to an existing church. The electrical system is 208Y/120 volts, 3-phase. What MINIMUM size THWN copper feeder conductors are required for the kitchen addition?

A. 1 AWG
B. 1/0 AWG
C. 2/0 AWG
D. 3/0 AWG

36. A feeder at a school welding shop is to supply the following listed transformer arc welders all with a 50 percent duty cycle.

   two (2) with 60 amperes rated primary current
   two (2) with 50 amperes rated primary current
   two (2) with 40 amperes rated primary current

The feeder is required to have an ampacity of at LEAST _____.

A. 213 amperes
B. 196 amperes
C. 182 amperes
D. 176 amperes

37. The National Electrical Code® requires ventilation of a battery room where batteries are being charged to prevent:

A. battery corrosion.
B. electrostatic charge.
C. deterioration of the building steel.
D. an accumulation of an explosive mixture.

38. What is the MAXIMUM balanced demand load, in VA, permitted to be connected to a new service of a commercial building, given the following conditions?

   The service is 208Y/120 volts, 3-phase, with a 600 ampere rated main circuit breaker.
   The maximum load must not exceed 80 percent of the ampere rating of the main circuit breaker.

A. 57,600 VA
B. 99,840 VA
C. 172,923 VA
D. 178,692 VA

39. Determine the MAXIMUM standard size overcurrent protection required for the primary and secondary side of a transformer, when primary and secondary overcurrent protection is to be provided, given the following related information.

   150 kVA rating
   Primary - 480 volt, 3-phase, 3-wire
   Secondary - 208Y/120 volt, 3-phase, 4-wire

A. Primary - 500 amperes, Secondary - 500 amperes
B. Primary - 450 amperes, Secondary - 600 amperes
C. Primary - 500 amperes, Secondary - 450 amperes
D. Primary - 450 amperes, Secondary - 500 amperes

40. Openings around electrical penetrations of a wall of a designated information technology room are required to be _____ .

A. insulated
B. airtight
C. firestopped
D. sound proof

41. When buried raceways pass under a driveway, the MINIMUM cover requirements _____ .

A. decrease if installed in rigid metal conduit (RMC).
B. do not change in regard to wiring methods used.
C. shall be increased for direct burial cables.
D. can be increased, decreased, or remain the same, depending on the wiring method used.

42. Which one of the following listed is NOT permitted to be installed with service-entrance conductors in a service-entrance raceway?

A. grounding conductors
B. load management control conductors
C. feeders extending to another building
D. equipment bonding jumpers

43. Where used outside of a, building, aluminum or copper-clad aluminum grounding electrode conductors shall not be terminated WITHIN_____ of the earth.

A. 18 inches
B. 24 inches
C. 3 feet
D. 6 feet

44. Where installed for a commercial occupancy, determine the MINIMUM size THWN copper conductors required from the terminals of a 3-phase, 277/480 volt, 4-wire, 200 kW generator to the first distribution device(s) containing overcurrent protection, where the design and operation of the generator does NOT prevent overloading.

A. 250 kcmil
B. 300 kcmil
C. 400 kcmil
D. 500 kcmil

45. Enclosures containing circuit breakers, switches and motor controllers located in Class II, Division 2 locations, shall be _____ or otherwise identified for the location.

A. gastight
B. vapor-proof
C. dusttight
D. stainless steel

46. Information technology equipment is permitted to be connected to a branch circuit by flexible cord-and-attachment plug cap, if the cord does NOT exceed _____ in length.

A. 6 feet
B. 8 feet
C. 10 feet
D. 15 feet

47. Where required, conduit seals installed in Class I, Division 1 & 2 locations shall have the minimum thickness of the sealing compound not less than the trade size of the sealing fitting and, in no case less than _____.

A. 1/2 in.
B. 5/8 in.
C. 3/4 in.
D. 1 in.

48. Given: A one-family dwelling to be built will have 4,000 sq. ft. of livable space, a 600 sq. ft. garage, a 400 sq. ft. open porch, a 2,000 sq. ft. unfinished basement (adaptable for future use), three (3) small-appliance branch-circuits and a branch circuit for the laundry room. Determine the demand load, in VA, on the ungrounded service-entrance conductors for the general lighting and receptacle loads using the standard method of calculation for a one-family dwelling.

A. 10,350 VA
B. 9,825 VA
C. 7,350 VA
D. 24,000 VA

49. Determine the MINIMUM size Type SOW flexible cord that may be used to supply a 30 hp, 3-phase, 480-volt, continuous-duty, ac motor from the motor controller to the motor terminations. Assume voltage-drop and elevated ambient temperature are not considerations.

A. 4 AWG
B. 6 AWG
C. 8 AWG
D. 10 AWG

50. Portable structures for fairs, carnivals and similar events shall not be located under or within a MINIMUM of _____ horizontally of conductors operating in excess of 600 volts.

A. 22½ feet
B. 15 feet
C. 10 feet
D. 12 feet

51. Flexible cord and cables shall be permitted to be attached to building surfaces _____.

A. under no circumstances
B. where concealed
C. where used as a substitute for the fixed wiring of a structure
D. where the length of the cord or cable from a busway plug-in device to a **suitable tension "take-up" support device does not exceed 6 feet**

52. In regard to outside branch circuits of overhead spans of open individual conductors for 600 volts or less up to 50 feet in length, the NEC® mandates the conductors to be NOT less than _____ copper in size

A. 12 AWG
B. 10 AWG
C. 8 AWG
D. 6 AWG

53. As defined in the NEC®, a controller is any switch or device that is normally used to _____.

A. start and stop a motor by making and breaking the motor circuit current
B. start and stop a motor by making and breaking the control circuit current
C. control a motor by making and breaking the overload circuit current
D. disconnect or start a motor by any means

54. The MINIMUM spacing required between live bare metal parts in feeder circuits of 480 volt industrial control panels and bare metal parts of the enclosure is _____.

A. 1/2 in.
B. 3/4 in.
C. 1 in.
D. 1¼ in.

55. AFCI protection is required for all 15- and 20-ampere, 120-volt, branch circuits supplying outlets located in _____ .

A. boat houses
B. recreational vehicles
C. all guest rooms and suites of hotels
D. guest rooms and guest suites of hotels that are provided with permanent provisions for cooking

56. All swimming pool electric water heaters shall have the heating elements subdivided into loads not exceeding 48 amperes and protected at NOT over _____ .

A. 45 amperes
B. 50 amperes
C. 55 amperes
D. 60 amperes

57. In regard to emergency and legally required standby systems, transfer switches shall be _____ and approved by the authority having jurisdiction.

A. manual
B. automatic
C. nonautomatic
D. red in color

58. Where Type SE service-entrance cable is used for interior wiring as a substitute for Type NM cable for branch circuits and feeders, where installed in thermal insulation, the ampacity shall be in accordance with the _____ conductor temperature rating.

A. 40º C
B. 60º C
C. 75º C
D. 90º C

59. Power distribution blocks shall be permitted in pull and junction boxes having a volume over _____ for connections of conductors where installed in boxes, provided the power distribution blocks do not have uninsulated live parts exposed within the box, whether or not the box cover is exposed.

A. 50 cu. in.
B. 75 cu. in.
C. 100 cu. in.
D. 1650 cu. in.

60. Where a receptacle outlet is removed from an underfloor raceway, the conductors supplying the outlet shall be _____ .

A. capped with an approved insulating material
B. taped off with red colored tape
C. marked and identified
D. removed from the raceway

61. What is the MINIMUM dimension required by the NEC® for a working space containing live parts on both sides of the equipment that will require examination and maintenance of the equipment when energized and operating at 480-volts between conductors?

A. 4 feet
B. 3 feet
C. 6 feet
D. 5 feet

62. Where a mobile home park has 25 mobile home lots calculated at 15,000 VA each, determine the MINIMUM required ampacity required for the ungrounded service-entrance conductors.

A. 400 amperes
B. 380 amperes
C. 820 amperes
D. 782 amperes

63. A 3-phase, 150 kVA transformer with a 208Y/120 volt secondary has an existing load of 212 amperes on each of the ungrounded phases. What is the MAXIMUM load, in amperes, that may be added to each of the ungrounded secondary phases?

A. 416 amperes
B. 180 amperes
C. 204 amperes
D. 250 amperes

64. In regard to an isolated grounding type receptacle, the reason the insulated isolated grounding conductor is not bonded to the outlet box is _____ .

A. for the reduction of electrical noise
B. to insure the circuit breaker will trip in the event of a ground-fault
C. to prevent the circuit breaker from tripping in the event of a ground-fault
D. for the reduction of voltage-drop

65. Where a central vacuum assembly is located in a storage closet adjacent to the laundry room of a dwelling, accessible non-current-carrying metal parts of the assembly likely to be energized shall be _____ .

A. isolated
B. insulated
C. GFCI protected
D. connected to an equipment grounding conductor

66. Type CMP communications cable of NOT more than _____ in length shall be permitted in ducts used for environmental air if they are directly associated with the air distribution system.

A. 8 feet
B. 6 feet
C. 4 feet
D. 2 feet

67. The disconnecting switch or circuit breaker for electric signs and outline lighting systems shall open all _____ conductors simultaneously on multi-wire branch circuits supplying the sign or outline lighting system.

A. grounded and ungrounded
B. grounded, ungrounded and grounding
C. grounding, ungrounded and bonding
D. ungrounded

68. In an industrial establishment, what is the MAXIMUM length of 200 ampere rated busway that may be tapped to a 600 ampere rated busway, without additional overcurrent protection?

A. 10 feet
B. 25 feet
C. 50 feet
D. 75 feet

69. Where constant wattage heating cables are installed in concrete floors, the cables shall NOT exceed _____ per linear foot per cable.

A. 30 watts
B. 54 watts
C. 16½ watts
D. 37 watts

70. In general, the NEC® does not mandate the maximum number of circuit breakers a panelboard may contain. An exception to this rule is _____, which is limited to no more than 42 overcurrent protection devices.

A. a delta-connected panelboard
B. a split-bus panelboard
C. a 3-phase panelboard
D. panelboards containing overcurrent protection devices rated only 30 amperes or less

71. When water reaches the height of the established electrical datum plane for an irrigation pond, the service equipment must _____.

A. be installed in a NEMA 6 enclosure
B. float
C. be installed in a NEMA 6P enclosure
D. disconnect

72. In health care facilities, essential electrical systems shall have a MINIMUM _____.

A. capacity of 200 gallons of fuel for the auxiliary generator
B. of two independent sources of power
C. of 1 hour back-up time
D. capacity of 150 kVA

73. Lampholders shall be constructed, installed, or equipped with shades or guards so that combustible material is not subjected to temperatures in EXCESS of _____.

A. 130 degrees F
B. 140 degrees F
C. 162 degrees F
D. 194 degrees F

74. Pendant conductors having a length of at LEAST _____ or more, shall be twisted together where not cabled in a listed assembly.

A. 3 feet
B. 4 feet
C. 5 feet
D. 6 feet

75. When installed in a metal enclosure, the grounding electrode conductor for a surge-protective device (SPD) or transient voltage suppressor (TVSS) of 1 kV or less, shall be _____.

A. a minimum size of 12 AWG copper
B. a minimum size of 6 AWG
C. removed
D. bonded to both ends of the enclosure

76. At least one structural member of a building or structure that is direct contact with the earth for at LEAST _____ or more, with or without concrete encasement shall be permitted to be used as a grounding electrode.

A. 20 feet
B. 8 feet
C. 10 feet
D. 6 feet

77. The circuit supplying an autotransformer-type dimmer installed in theaters and similar places shall NOT exceed _____ between conductors.

A. 480 volts
B. 277 volts
C. 250 volts
D. 150 volts

78. At least one receptacle outlet shall be installed within 18 inches of the top of a show window of a retail store for each _____ of show window area measured horizontally.

A. 8 linear ft.
B. 10 linear ft.
C. 12 linear ft.
D. 15 linear ft.

79. Each luminaire installed in Class III, Divisions 1 and 2 locations shall be clearly marked to show the maximum wattage of the lamps that shall be permitted without exceeding an exposed surface temperature of _____ under normal conditions of use.

A. 329° F
B. 165° F
C. 144° F
D. 125° F

80. Conductors supplying a continuous-rated, varying-duty motor shall have an ampacity of NOT less than _____ of the motor nameplate current rating.

A. 125 percent
B. 140 percent
C. 150 percent
D. 200 percent

81. What is the MAXIMUM spacing allowed for supporting Type MC cable where used as a branch circuit in a manufactured wiring system?

A. 3 feet
B. 5 feet
C. 6 feet
D. 10 feet

82. Receptacles or receptacle cover plates supplied from the emergency system in a hospital, shall be identified by _____ .

A. brown in color
B. white in color
C. distinctive color or marking
D. an orange triangle

83. What is the MAXIMUM standard size circuit breaker that may be used for overcurrent protection of size 4/0 AWG THWN copper conductors that are not serving a motor load?

A. 200 amperes
B. 225 amperes
C. 230 amperes
D. 250 amperes

84. A multiwire branch circuit supplying a motor fuel dispensing pump, shall be provided with a switch that will disconnect _____ .

A. only one ungrounded supply conductor
B. all of the ungrounded supply conductors only
C. only the neutral (grounded) conductor
D. the grounded conductor and all of the ungrounded supply conductors

85. The depth of the working space in front of a 120-volt, single-phase, fire alarm control panel (FACP) is required to be at LEAST _____.

A. 2½ feet
B. 3 feet
C. 3½ feet
D. 4 feet

86. Where an air conditioning unit is supplied with size 6 AWG CU conductors and protected by a 60 ampere circuit breaker, the MINIMUM size CU equipment grounding conductor permitted for this installation is _____.

A. 12 AWG
B. 10 AWG
C. 8 AWG
D. 6 AWG

87. Which of the following is NOT required to be marked on the nameplate of a transformer?

A. overcurrent protection
B. manufacturer
C. kVA rating
D. voltage

88. When combination surface nonmetallic raceways are used for both signaling and for power and lighting circuits, the different systems shall be _____.

A. prohibited
B. run in the same compartment
C. run in separate compartments
D. maintain a spacing of at least ½ in.

89. Where explosionproof equipment is provided with metric threaded entries, which of the following methods is approved to adapt the entries from metric threads to NPT threads?

A. Approved adapters from metric threads to NPT threads shall be used.
B. Tap the metric threaded entries to NPT threads.
C. Thread the conduit with metric threads.
D. All of these are approved methods.

90. An indoor located 100 kVA, dry-type transformer with a 4,160 volt primary is required to have a clearance of at LEAST _____ from combustible material.

A. 6 inches
B. 10 inches
C. 12 inches
D. 8 inches

91. A clearance of NOT less than _____ must be maintained from the maximum water level of a permanently installed swimming pool and messenger-supported *tri-plex* service-drop conductors of 0-750 volts.

A. 10 feet
B. 14½ feet
C. 19 feet
D. 22½ feet

92. Where an apartment complex has a calculated connected lighting load of 205.4 kVA, what is the DEMAND load, in kVA, on the ungrounded service-entrance conductors where applying the standard (general) method of calculation? Given: Each dwelling unit in the complex has cooking facilities provided.

A. 58.9 kVA
B. 60.2 kVA
C. 16.5 kVA
D. 65.3 kVA

93. Small wind electric systems, where connected to utility sources, shall comply with the requirements of _____ of the NEC®.

A. Article 800
B. Article 705
C. Article 690
D. Article 700

94. For the purpose of sizing branch circuits for fixed storage-type water heaters with a capacity of 120 gallons or less, the water heater shall be considered _____ .

A. a continuous load
B. an intermittent load
C. a noncontinuous load
D. a short-time load

95. When supplying a 36,000 VA, 240-volt, single-phase load in an area where the ambient temperature reaches 119º F, determine the MINIMUM size 75º C rated copper conductors required to supply the load.

A. 1/0 AWG
B. 2/0 AWG
C. 3/0 AWG
D. 4/0 AWG

96. Color coding shall be permitted to identify intrinsically safe conductors where they are colored _____ and where no other conductors of the same color are used.

A. light blue
B. orange
C. yellow
D. purple

97. What is the MINIMUM bend radius of trade size 4 in. rigid metal conduit (RMC) where the bend is not made with a one-shot or full-shoe bender?

A. 16 inches
B. 18 inches
C. 24 inches
D. 30 inches

98. Where exceptions are not to be applied, determine the MINIMUM required length of a junction box that has a trade size 3½ in. conduit containing four (4) size 250 kcmil conductors, pulled through the box for a 90º angle pull.

A. 21 inches
B. 24 inches
C. 28 inches
D. 34 inches

99. An approved method of protection for equipment installed in Class I, Zone 0, hazardous locations is _____ .

A. purged and pressurized
B. encapsulation
C. powder filling
D. oil immersion

100. Cables over 600 volts and those rated 600 volts or less, are permitted to be installed in a common cable tray without a fixed barrier, where the cables over 600 volts are _____ .

A. Type MI
B. Type AC
C. Type CT
D. Type MC

END OF MASTER ELECTRICIANS FINAL EXAM

Answer Key
&
NEC® References

MAINTENANCE ELECTRICIAN
PRACTICE EXAM #1
ANSWER KEY

ANSWER	REFERENCE	NEC PG.#
1. A	Art. 100	pg. 33
2. B	Art. 100	pg. 27
3. A	Art. 100	pg. 30
4. B	General Knowledge	
5. A	General Knowledge	
6. C	Trade Knowledge	
7. B	358.26	pg. 218
8. D	Tbl. 430.248	pg. 337
9. D	Art. 100	pg. 29
10. B	110.12(A)	pg. 35
11. C	110.26(A)(3)	pg. 38
12. D	310.106(C)	pg. 172
13. C	Trade Knowledge	
14. C	240.6(A)	pg. 91
15. B	Tbl. 314.16(A)	pg. 179
16. D	362.30(A)	pg. 221
17. D	210.21(B)(1)	pg. 54
18. C	430.6(A)(1) Tbl. 430.248 430.22	pg. 311 pg. 337 pg. 316

FLC of 7½ hp motor = 40 amps x 125% = 50 amperes

19. A	Tbl. 310.15(B)(16)	pg. 154

20. B   240.60(D)   pg. 97

21. C   Single-phase current formula

$$I = P \div E \quad I = \frac{10 \text{ kW} \times 1000}{240 \text{ volts}} = \frac{10{,}000}{240} = 41.6 \text{ amperes}$$

22. A   Art. 100   pg. 26

23. B   Tbl. 310.104(A)   pg. 169
                Tbl. 310.15(B)(16)   pg. 154

24. B   Single-phase current Formula

$$I = P \div E \quad I = \frac{150 \text{ watts} \times 15}{120 \text{ volts}} = \frac{2250}{120} = 18.75 \text{ amperes}$$

25. D   404.8(A)   pg. 267 & 268

##

MAINTENANCE ELECTRICIAN
PRACTICE EXAM #2
ANSWER KEY

ANSWER	REFERENCE	NEC PG.#
1. B	110.14(C)	pg. 36
	Tbl. 310.15(B)(16)	pg. 154

*NOTE: When a conductor is connected to a termination that has a temperature rating lower than that of the conductor then, the conductor ampacity rating is based on the lower value.

2. B	Trade Knowledge	
3. A	90.1(B)	pg. 22
4. C	Art. 100	pg. 28
5. B	Trade Knowledge	
6. C	Trade Knowledge	
7. D	110.15	pg. 36
8. B	Annex C, Tbl. C.1	pg. 746
9. B	Tbl. 310.15(B)(3)(a)	pg. 152
10. B	300.20(A)	pg. 144
11. A	358.30(A)	pg. 219
12. B	Tbl. 310.15(B)(2)(a)	pg. 150
13. C	430.6(A)(2)	pg. 312
14. A	430.22	pg. 316
15. C	Trade Knowledge	
16. C	240.83(D)	pg. 97

Copyright© 2016

17. A   Single-Phase Current Formula
$$I = P \div E$$

$$I = \frac{15 \text{ kW} \times 1{,}000}{208 \text{ volts}} = \frac{15{,}000}{208} = 72 \text{ amperes}$$

18. A   200.7(A)(2)   pg. 47

19. C   Three-Phase Current Formula
$$I = P \div E \times 1.732$$

$$I = \frac{9 \text{ kW} \times 1000}{208 \times 1.732} = \frac{9{,}000}{360.25} = 24.9 \text{ amperes}$$

20. B   Chpt. 9, Tbl. 8   pg. 721
                    Distance Formula

1st. find allowable VD - 240 volts x 3% = 7.2 volts

$$D = \frac{CM \times VD}{2 \times K \times I} \quad D = \frac{16{,}510 \times 7.2}{2 \times 12.9 \times 42} = \frac{118{,}872}{1{,}083.6} = 109.7 \text{ feet}$$

21. B   348.20(A)(2)c.   pg. 206

22. D   110.26(A)(2)   pg. 38

23. A   210.19(A)(1)   pg. 52

24. C   Tbl. 210.21(B)(3)   pg. 54
                    Tbl. 210.24   pg. 55

25. B   240.4(D)(5)   pg. 90

##

RESIDENTIAL ELECTRICIAN
PRACTICE EXAM #3
ANSWER KEY

ANSWER	RERERENCE	NEC PG.#
1. B	210.11(C)(3)	pg. 52
2. C	210.12(B)	pg. 52
3. C	680.71	pg. 590
4. C	410.16(C)(1)	pg. 281
5. A	210.50(C)	pg. 55
6. D	230.90	pg. 86
7. C	422.11(E)(3)	pg. 291
	240.6(A)	pg. 91
	Single-Phase Current Formula	

$I = P \div E$ I = 4500 VA ÷ 240 V = 18.75 amps x 150% = 28.1 amperes
*NOTE: The next size circuit breaker with a rating of 30 amperes should be selected.

8. A	410.117(C)	pg. 286
9. A	550.10(A)	pg. 482
10. B	210.11(C)(1)&(2)	pg. 52
	220.52(A)&(B)	pg. 65

2 - small appliance circuits @ 1,500 VA ea. = 3,000 VA
1 laundry circuit @ 1,500 VA = 1,500 VA
TOTAL = 4,500 VA

11. C	210.63	pg. 58
12. C	Tbl. 220.12	pg. 63

70 ft. x 30 ft. = 2100 sq. ft. x 3 VA = 6300 VA (house)
120 volts x 15 amperes = 1800 VA (one circuit)

$$\frac{6300 \text{ VA (house)}}{1800 \text{ VA (one circuit)}} = 3.5 = 4 \text{ circuits}$$

Copyright© 2016

13. B	210.8(A)(2)	pg. 50
14. D	230.9(A)	pg. 79
15. C	Trade Knowledge Single-Phase Current Formula	

100 watts x 6 luminaires = 600 watts total
I = P ÷ E   I = 600 watts ÷ 120 volts = 5 amperes

16. B	230.24(B)(1)	pg. 80
17. C	314.29	pg. 184
18. A	210.52(A)(2)(1)	pg. 56
19. B	312.2	pg. 174
20. A	210.52(H)	pg. 58
21. A	210.52(C)(1)	pg. 56
22. B	Tbl. 300.5, Col. 4	pg. 138
23. C	334.15(C)	pg. 197
24. A	200.6(B)(4)	pg. 46
25. B	404.2(A)	pg. 266

##

RESIDENTIAL ELECTRICIAN
PRACTICE EXAM #4
ANSWER KEY

ANSWER	REFERENCE	NEC PG.#
1. C	210.52(C)(5)	pg. 57
2. D	240.24(E)	pg. 95
3. B	255.18(2)	pg. 72
4. D	Trade knowledge	

120 volts x 15 amperes = 1,800 VA (one circuit)
9,600 VA (load) ÷ 1,800 VA (one circuit) = 5.3 = 6 circuits

5. B	210.8(A)(6)	pg. 50
6. B	314.16(B)(1),(2),(4)&(5)	pg. 178
	Tbl. 314.16(B)	pg. 179

```
Size 14 AWG  = 2.00 cu. in. x 4  =  8.00 cubic inches
Size 12 AWG  = 2.25 cu. in. x 4  =  9.00 cubic inches
equip grnd.  = 2.25 cu. in. x 1  =  2.25 cubic inches
clamps       = 2.25 cu. in. x 1  =  2.25 cubic inches
recept.      = 2.25 cu. in. x 2  =  4.50 cubic inches
switch       = 2.00 cu. in. x 2  =  4.00 cubic inches
                          TOTAL  =30.00 cubic inches
```

COMMENT: Clamps, 1 or more, are counted as equal to the largest wire in the box. [314.16(B)(2)] Equipment grounding conductors, 1 or more, are counted as equal to the largest equipment grounding conductor in the box. [314.16(B)(5)] Devices are counted as equal to two (2) conductors, based on the largest conductor connected to the device. [314.16(B)(4)]

7. C	680.22(A)(1)	pg. 579
8. B	240.24(F)	pg. 95
9. B	210.23(A)(1)	pg. 54

20 amps x 80% = 16 amperes

10. D	210.11(C)(2)	pg. 52

Copyright© 2016

11. C	230.79(C)	pg. 85
12. A	Tbl. 220.55 & Note 3	pg. 66

    Use column B - 5 appliances = 45% demand
    6 kW + 8 kW + 3.5 kW + 6 kW + 3.5 kW = 27 kW (total connected load)
    27 kW x 45% = 12.15 kW (demand load)

13. C	550.32(C)	pg. 489
14. D	225.19(B)	pg. 73
15. B	Tbl. 250.66	pg. 115
	250.66(B)	pg. 115
16. C	590.3(B)	pg. 516
17. B	314.16(B)(3)	pg. 178
18. C	424.3(A)	pg. 296
19. B	358.30(A)	pg. 219
20. D	230.71(A)	pg. 84
21. A	340.80	pg. 201
22. A	314.20	pg. 180
23. B	210.8(A)(7)	pg. 50
24. A	210.52(B)(2)	pg. 56
	210.11(C)(2)&(3)	pg. 52
25. C	250.52(A)(1)	pg. 111

###

RESIDENTIAL ELECTRICIAN
PRACTICE EXAM #5
ANSWER KEY

ANSWER	REFERENCE	NEC PG.#
1. D	422.16(B)(2)(1)	pg. 292
2. B	Tbl. 310.15(B)(7)	pg. 153
3. C	314.27(C)	pg. 183
4. B	250.68(A),EX.1	pg. 115
5. A	230.23(B)	pg. 80
6. C	Tbl. 314.16(A)	pg. 179
7. C	220.12 Tbl. 220.12	pg. 61 pg. 63

2600 sq. ft. x 3 VA = 7800 VA (total lighting VA of house)
120 volts x 15 amperes = 1800 VA (one circuit)

$$\frac{7800 \text{ VA (load)}}{1800 \text{ VA (one circuit)}} = 4.3 = 5 \text{ lighting circuits}$$

8. A	220.14(J)(1)	pg. 63
9. D	440.62(C)	pg. 346
10. B	220.53	pg. 65
11. D	210.52(D)	pg. 57
12. C	300.4(D)	pg. 137
13. B	Power Formula	

P = I x E   P = 30 amps x 240 volts = 7,200 VA

14. D	Tbl. 310.104(A) 310.10(B)&(C)(2)	pg. 170 pg. 147 & 148
15. B	210.52(C)(1)	pg. 56
16. C	220.54	pg. 65

Copyright© 2016

17. C   210.23(B)   pg. 54 & 55

    30 amperes x 80% = 24 amperes

18. A   210.8(A)(6)   pg. 50

19. D   Tbl. 220.55 & Note 3   pg. 66

    Use column B - 2 appliances = 65% demand
    5 kW + 7 kW = 12 kW (total connected load)
    12 kW x 65% (demand) = 7.8 kW (demand load)

20. A   Tbl. 250.122   pg. 125

21. A   210.6(A)(1)   pg. 49

22. D   424.3(B)   pg. 296
              210.19(A)(1)   pg. 52

23. D   250.53(G)   pg. 113

24. B   410.116(A)(1)   pg. 286

25. A   334.12(B)(4)   pg. 197

##

RESIDENTIAL ELECTRICIAN
PRACTICE EXAM #6
ANSWER KEY

ANSWER	REFERENCE	NEC PG.#
1. A	Art. 100 - Def.	pg. 30
2. B	230.26	pg. 80
3. C	Tbl. 110.26(A)(1)	pg. 38
4. C	230.28	pg. 80
5. A	680.43(C)	pg. 587
6. C	680.22(A)(4)	pg. 579
7. D	314.27(A)(1)&(2)	pg. 182
8. B	Tbl. 430.248	pg. 337
9. C	250.53(G)	pg. 113
10. D	406.9(C)	pg. 273
11. D	Tbl. 400.5(A)(1),Col. B	pg. 258
12. C	680.42(A)(2)	pg. 586
13. B	426.4 210.19(A)(1) 210.20(A)	pg. 304 pg. 52 pg. 53
14. B	Tbl. 300.5, Col. 2	pg. 138
15. C	210.70(A)(2)(c)	pg. 58
16. D	Tbl. 352.30	pg. 210
17. A	300.16(A)	pg. 142
18. D	422.11(E)(1)&(3)	pg. 291
19. B	394.10(1)	pg. 246

Copyright© 2016

20. D	210.8(A)(7)	pg. 50
21. A	334.24	pg. 197
22. C	Tbl. 314.16(B)	pg. 179
23. B	334.30	pg. 197
24. A	230.31(B)	pg. 81
25. B	Tbl. 314.16(B)	pg. 179
	314.16(B)(4)	pg. 178

18 cu. in. (box)/2.25 cu. in.(#12 wire) = 8 wires (allowable fill)
- <u>2 wires (device)</u>
6 wires may be installed

*NOTE: A size 12/2 AWG with ground NM cable contains three (3) conductors.

<u>6 wires (may be added)</u>
3 (wires in NM cable)   = 2 size 12/2 NM cables may be installed

##

JOURNEYMAN ELECTRICIAN
PRACTICE EXAM #7
ANSWER KEY

ANSWER	REFERENCE	NEC PG.#
1. C	250.53(B)	pg. 112
2. B	250.102(C) Tbl. 250.66	pg. 118 pg. 115
3. A	502.10(B)(4)	pg. 387
4. D	300.5(B)	pg. 137
5. D	Tbl. 310.15(B)(16) Tbl. 310.15(B)(3)(a)	pg. 154 pg. 152

Size 1/0 AWG THW ampacity = 150 amperes before derating
150 amperes x 80% (adjustment factor) = 120 amperes

6. A	Art. 100	pg. 27
7. C	430.22 Tbl. 310.15(B)(16)	pg. 316 pg. 154

FLC of motor = 70 amperes x 125% = 87.5 amperes
Size 3 AWG THW with an ampacity of 100 amperes should be selected.

8. C	240.4(B)(1),(2)&(3) 240.6(A)	pg. 90 pg. 91
9. B	Tbl. 430.250	pg. 338
10. A	525.21(A)	pg. 471
11. B	Annex C, Tbl. C.1	pg. 746
12. B	215.3	pg. 60

240 amperes x 125% = 300 amperes

13. C	350.30(A)	pg. 208

Copyright© 2016

14. C   314.28(A)(1)   pg. 183

15. D   Chpt. 9, Note 4 to Tbls.   pg. 711

16. C   Tbl. 348.22   pg. 206

17. D   680.23(B)(2)   pg. 581

18. C   680.10   pg. 577

19. A   700.12(A)   pg. 624

20. C   Tbl. 110.26(A)(1)   pg. 38

21. B   210.60(B)   pg. 58

22. B   410.68   pg. 285

23. C   300.4(G)   pg. 137

24. C   500.5(D)   pg. 371

25. A   Single-Phase Current Formula
$I = P \div E$

$$\frac{15 \text{ kVA} \times 1{,}000}{240 \text{ volts}} = \frac{15{,}000}{240} = 62.50 \text{ amperes}$$

###

JOURNEYMAN ELECTRICIAN
PRACTICE EXAM #8
ANSWER KEY

ANSWER	REFERENCE	NEC. PG.#
1. A	Note to Tbl. 430.22(E) 430.33	pg. 317 pg. 320
2. D	430.84,Ex.	pg. 328
3. D	220.14(I)	pg. 63
4. D	Tbl. 310.104(A) Tbl. 310.15(B)(16)	pg. 169 pg. 154
5. B	250.112(M)	pg. 121
6. A	517.64(A)(1),(2)&(3)	pg. 455
7. A	Tbl. 310.15(B)(17)	pg. 155
8. C	314.16(B)(4)	pg. 178
9. D	430.6(A)(1)	pg. 311
10. C	220.14(F) 600.5(B) 210.19(A)(1)	pg. 62 pg. 519 pg. 52

1,200 VA x 125% = 1,500 VA

11. A	Annex C, Tbl. C.10(A)	pg. 794
12. C	422.11(C)	pg. 291
13. A	500.5(B)	pg. 369
14. D	300.6(D)	pg. 140
15. C	210.3	pg. 48
16. D	424.22(B)	pg. 297
17. B	645.5(B)(1)	pg. 561
18. C	332.30	pg. 195
19. A	314.24(A)	pg. 182

Copyright© 2016

20. A   300.5(D)(1)   pg. 139

21. B   Tbl. 250.122   pg. 125

22. C   230.95   pg. 87

23. A   Tbl. 310.15(B)(16)   pg. 154
                 Tbl. 310.15(B)(2)(a)   pg. 150
                 Tbl. 310.15(B)(3)(a)   pg. 152

Size 500 KCMIL THWN copper ampacity before derating = 380 amperes
380 amperes x .67 (temp. correction) x .7 (adjustment factor) = 178.22 amperes

24. C   348.20(A)(2)c.   pg. 206
                 410.117(C)   pg. 286

25. C   501.15(C)(3)   pg. 379

##

JOURNEYMAN ELECTRICIAN
PRACTICE EXAM #9
ANSWER KEY

ANSWER	REFERENCE	NEC PG.#
1. D	362.12(5)	pg. 221
2. C	Tbl. 430.250	pg. 338
3. D	324.10(B)(2)	pg. 189
4. C	200.6(D)(2)	pg. 47
5. D	376.56	pg. 232
6. A	352.26	pg. 209
7. B	250.52(A)(5)(a)	pg. 112
8. D	350.12(1)	pg. 207
9. B	110.14(C)	pg. 36
	310.15(A)(2)	pg. 149
	Tbl. 310.15(B)(16)	pg. 154
	Tbl. 310.15(B)(2)(a)	pg. 150

Size 3 AWG THHN ampacity before derating = 110 amperes (90 deg. C Col.)
110 amperes x .96 (temperature correction) = 105.6 amperes

*NOTE: Size 3 AWG (60 deg. C Col.) with an allowable ampacity of 85 amperes should be selected.

10. D	800.44(B)	pg. 671
11. B	Tbl. 352.30	pg. 210
12. A	250.24(C)	pg. 105
13. B	392.10(B)(1)(a)	pg. 240
14. B	440.64	pg. 346
15. A	210.8(B)(2)	pg. 51
16. D	Current Formula & Ohms Law	

$I = P \div E$ $I = 100$ watts $\div 120$ volts $= .833$ amperes
$R = E \div I$ $R = 120$ volts $\div .833$ amperes $= 144.05$ ohms

17. D	430.24(1)&(2)	pg. 318
18. A	Tbl. 250.122	pg. 125
19. B	430.102(B)(2),Ex.	pg. 330
20. C	590.6(B)(2)(a)(1)	pg. 518
21. A	Tbl. 250.66	pg. 115

Size 500 kcmil x 4 conductors = 2,000 kcmil total area
*NOTE: Aluminum service-entrance conductors over 1750 kcmil require a size 3/0 AWG copper grounding electrode conductor.

22. B	Tbl. 630.11(A)	pg. 552
	Tbl. 310.15(B)(16)	pg. 154

.78 (duty cycle) x 50 amperes (primary current) = 39 amperes
*NOTE: Tbl. 310.15(B)(16) indicates size 8 AWG conductors should be selected.

23. C	647.1	pg. 563
24. B	517.19(B)(1)&(2)	pg. 444
25. B	400.8(2)	pg. 260

##

JOURNEYMAN ELECTRICIAN
PRACTICE EXAM #10
ANSWER KEY

ANSWER	REFERENCE	NEC PG.#
1. A	424.44(G)	pg. 300
2. A	406.10(B)(1)	pg. 273
3. A	680.21(A)(5)	pg. 579
4. D	250.53(H)	pg. 113
5. C	240.40	pg. 96
6. D	Chpt. 9, Tbl. 8 Voltage-drop formula	pg. 721

$$VD = \frac{2KID}{CM} \quad VD = \frac{2 \times 12.9 \times 80 \text{ amps} \times 200 \text{ ft.}}{52,620 \text{ CM}} = 7.84 \text{ volts}$$

7. B	501.15(A)(1)	pg. 378
8. B	110.3(B)	pg. 35
9. D	Tbl. 514.3(B)(1)	pg. 426
10. B	517.31	pg. 447
11. A	725.179(H)	pg. 649
12. B	Trade & General Knowledge 3-Phase Current Formula	

$$I = \frac{kVA \times 1,000}{E \times 1.732} \quad I = \frac{90 \times 1,000}{208 \times 1.732} = \frac{90,000}{360.25} = 250 \text{ amperes}$$

13. C	680.26(B) 680.26(B)(1)(a)	pg. 583 pg. 584
14. D	310.15(B)(3)(c) Tbl. 310.15(B)(3)(c)	pg. 152 pg. 152
15. B	430.32(A)(1)	pg. 319
16. C	Tbl. 210.24	pg. 55

17. D   250.64(C)(1)   pg. 114

18. B   Tbl. 314.16(B)   pg. 179

   Size 12 AWG = 2.25 cu. in. x 6 (existing wire in box) = 13.5 cu. in.

   cu. in. (allowable fill of box) -13.5
   cu. in. (existing wire in box)
   cu. in. (remaining space available)

   cu. in. (remaining space) = 5.4 = 5 size 10 AWG wires may be added
          cu. in. (#10)

19. B   550.10(G)   pg. 483

20. D   511.7(A)(1)   pg. 421

21. D   500.5(C)   pg. 370

22. C   422.10(A)   pg. 291
                  422.13   pg. 292

23. A   422.11(B)   pg. 291

24. D   250.53(G)   pg. 113

25. C   Chpt. 9, Tbl. 4   pg. 713
                  Chpt. 9, Tbl. 5   pg. 717

   Size 1 AWG THW = .1901 sq. in. x 5 = .9505 sq. in.
   Size 3 AWG THW = .1134 sq. in. x 5 = .567 sq. in.
                          Total = 1.5175 sq. in.

   *NOTE: A trade size 2½ in. IMC with an allowable 40% fill of 2.054 sq. in. should
          Be selected.

##

JOURNEYMAN ELECTRICIAN
PRACTICE EXAM #11
ANSWER KEY

ANSWER	REFERENCE	NEC PG.#
1. D	430.6	pg. 311
2. B	409.102(B)	pg. 279
3. C	225.18(4)	pg. 73
4. B	555.19(A)(4)	pg. 515
5. A	550.32(F)	pg. 490
6. C	Tbl. 310.104(A)	pg. 170
	Tbl. 310.15(B)(16)	pg. 154
	Tbl. 310.15(B)(2)(a)	pg. 150

Size 6 AWG AL XHHW ampacity before derating = 55 amperes
55 amperes x .87 (temperature correction) = 47.85 amperes

7. A	501.15(C)(6)	pg. 379
8. C	480.9(C)	pg. 360
	Tbl. 110.26(A)(1)	pg. 38
9. C	Tbl. 300.5, Col. 1	pg. 138
10. B	330.30(D)(2)	pg. 194
11. B	760.41(B)	pg. 652
	760.121(B)	pg. 655
12. C	682.11	pg. 591
13. D	300.5(E)	pg. 139
14. C	250.112(I)	pg. 121
15. A	Single-Phase Current Formula	

$$I = \frac{power}{volts} \quad I = \frac{18 \text{ kW} \times 1{,}000}{240 \text{ volts}} = \frac{18{,}000}{240} = 75 \text{ amperes}$$

16. A	250.24(A)	pg. 104
17. A	504.10(A)	pg. 395
18. B	210.62	pg. 58

$$\frac{80 \text{ ft. (show window)}}{12 \text{ ft. (per receptacle)}} = 6.7 = 7 \text{ receptacles}$$

19. B	690.61	pg. 605
20. A	430.24(1)&(2)	pg. 318
	Tbl. 430.250	pg. 338
	Tbl. 310.15(B)(16)	pg. 154

```
15 hp FLC - 42 amperes x 125% = 52.5 amperes
7½ hp FLC - 22 amperes x 100% = 22.0 amperes
3 hp FLC – 9.6 amperes x 100% =  9.6 amperes
                          Total = 84.1 amperes
```

*NOTE: Size 4 AWG THWN conductors with an allowable ampacity of 85 amperes should be selected.

21. D	450.11	pg. 352
22. C	310.10(H)(2)(3)&(4)	pg. 149
23. C	310.15(B)(3)(c)	pg. 152
	Tbl. 310.15(B)(3)(c)	pg. 152
24. C	450.42	pg. 354
25. B	680.22(B)(1)	pg. 579

##

MASTER ELECTRICIAN
PRACTICE EXAM #12
ANSWER KEY

ANSWER	REFERENCE	NEC PG.#
1. C	690.42,IN	pg. 603
2. B	110.31	pg. 40
3. B	820.15	pg. 687
4. C	430.109(C)(2)	pg. 331

15 amperes x 80% = 12 amperes

5. C	220.14(I)	pg. 63

120 volts x 20 amps = 2,400 VA (circuit)
2,400 VA (circuit)/180 VA (one receptacle) = 13 outlets

6. B	110.26(D)	pg. 39
7. A	240.24(B)(1)	pg. 95
8. B	Tbl. 310.15(B)(16)	pg. 154
	Tbl. 310.15(B)(2)(a)	pg. 150
	Tbl. 310.15(B)(3)(a)	pg. 152

Size 250 kcmil THWN copper ampacity before derating = 255 amperes
255 amps x .82 (temp. correction) x .8 (adjustment factor) = 167.28 amperes

9. D	Tbl. 430.72(B)	pg. 327
10. D	240.83(B)	pg. 96
11. B	250.52(A)(4)	pg. 112

Copyright© 2016

12. C	310.15(B)(3)(c)	pg. 152
	Tbl. 310.15(B)(3)(c)	pg. 152
	Tbl. 310.15(B)(2)(a)	pg. 150
	Tbl. 310.15(B)(16)	pg. 154

```
outdoor ambient temperature = 100 deg. F
adder (3" above roof)       + 40 deg. F
              TOTAL   140 deg. F (for derating)
```

Size 8 AWG THWN ampacity (before derating) = 50 amperes 50 amperes x .58 (temp. correction) = 29 amperes

13. D	Tbl. 310.104(A)	pg. 168
14. A	645.15	pg. 562
15. B	Tbl. 220.12	pg. 63

12,000 sq. ft. x 3 VA = 36,000 VA (building)
120 volts x 15 amps = 1,800 VA (1 circuit)

$$\frac{36{,}000 \text{ VA (building)}}{1{,}800 \text{ VA (1 circuit)}} = 20 \text{ circuits}$$

16. C	700.12(A)	pg. 624
17. A	230.6(1)	pg. 79
18. B	513.3(B)	pg. 422
19. D	Chpt. 9, Tbl. 8	pg. 721
	Voltage-drop formula	

$$VD = \frac{2KID}{CM} \quad VD = \frac{2 \times 12.9 \times 90 \text{ amps} \times 225 \text{ ft.}}{52{,}620 \text{ CM}} = 9.92 \text{ volts dropped}$$

20. D	525.32	pg. 472
21. D	551.73	pg. 501
22. C	511.12	pg. 422
23. B	Tbl. 430.52, Note 1	pg. 323
24. C	Tbl. 408.5	pg. 275
25. C	250.102(D)	pg. 119
	250.122(C)	pg. 124
	Tbl. 250.122	pg. 125

##

MASTER ELECTRICIAN
PRACTICE EXAM #13
ANSWER KEY

ANSWER	REFERENCE	NEC PG.#
1. D	408.5	pg. 275
2. B	324.10(E)	pg. 189
	324.12(4)	pg. 189
3. C	540.13	pg. 477
4. D	424.20(A)(3)	pg. 297
5. B	800.100(D)	pg. 674
6. D	314.28(A)(1)	pg. 183

3 in. (largest conduit) x 8 = 24 inches

7. A	Art. 100	pg. 28
8. C	680.58	pg. 589
9. D	514.11(B)	pg. 429
10. A	312.6(B)(2)	pg. 174
	Tbl. 312.6(B)	pg. 176
11. D	Tbl. 430.250	pg. 338
	430.22	pg. 316
	Tbl. 310.15(B)(2)(a)	pg. 150
	Tbl. 310.15(B)(16)	pg. 154

25 hp motor FLC = 74.8 amperes x 125% = 93.5 amperes
93.5 amps /.75 (temperature correction) = 124.6 amperes

*NOTE: The wire size needs to be increased because of the elevated ambient temperature. Size 1 AWG THWN conductors with an allowable ampacity of 130 amperes should be selected.

12. B	430.4,Ex.	pg. 311
13. B	517.33(A)(5)	pg. 448

Copyright© 2016

14. D　　　　　　　　　Tbl. 220.55 & Note 1　　　　　pg. 66

　　19 kW − 12 kW = 7 kW x 5% = 35% increase in Column C
　　17 kW (4 appliances in Col. C) x 135% = 22.95 kW demand

15. C　　　　　　　　　Tbl. 220.103　　　　　　　　pg. 70

16. C　　　　　　　　　690.31(B)　　　　　　　　　pg. 601

17. B　　　　　　　　　551.71　　　　　　　　　　 pg. 500

18. D　　　　　　　　　675.11(A)&(C)　　　　　　　pg. 574

19. B　　　　　　　　　3-Phase Current Formula
　　　　　　　　　　　Tbl. 450.3(B)　　　　　　　 pg. 349
　　　　　　　　　　　240.6(A)　　　　　　　　　　pg. 91

$$I = \frac{kVA \times 1000}{208 \times 1.732} \quad I = \frac{25 \times 1{,}000}{208 \times 1.732} = \frac{25{,}000}{360.25} = 69.3 \text{ amperes}$$

　　69.3 amperes x 125% = 86.62 amperes

　　*NOTE: You are permitted to go up to the next standard size OCP device
　　　　　which has a rating of 90 amperes.

20. B　　　　　　　　　250.122(F)　　　　　　　　　pg. 124

21. B　　　　　　　　　410.154　　　　　　　　　　pg. 289

22. C　　　　　　　　　Tbl. 430.250　　　　　　　　pg. 338
　　　　　　　　　　　430.24(1)&(2)　　　　　　　pg. 318
　　　　　　　　　　　Tbl. 310.15(B)(16)　　　　　pg. 154

　　40 hp FLC = 52 amps x 100% = 52 amperes
　　50 hp FLC = 65 amps x 100% = 65 amperes
　　60 hp FLC = 77 amps x 125% = <u>96 amperes</u>
　　　　　　　　　　　　 Total = 213 amperes

　　*NOTE: Size 4/0 AWG THWN conductors with an ampacity of 230 amperes
　　　　　should be selected.

23. C　　　　　　　　　517.35(A)　　　　　　　　　pg. 449

24. A　　　　　　　　　511.3(C)(2)(a)　　　　　　 pg. 420

25. C Chpt. 9, Tbl. 8 pg. 721
3-phase wire size formula

*NOTE: 3% of 480 volts = .03 x 480 = 14.4 (voltage drop permitted)

$$CM = \frac{1.732 \times K \times I \times D}{VD\ permitted}$$

$$CM = \frac{1.732 \times 21.2 \times 100\ amps \times 390\ ft.}{14.4\ volts} = 99{,}446\ CM$$

*NOTE: Size 1/0 AWG conductors with a CMA of 105,600 should be selected.

###

MASTER ELECTRICIAN
PRACTICE EXAM #14
ANSWER KEY

ANSWER	REFERENCE	NEC PG.#
1. B	702.11(B)	pg. 631
2. D	370.5	pg. 227
	240.4(B)(1),(2),&(3)	pg. 90
	240.6(A)	pg. 91
3. C	240.21(B)&(B)(2)(1)	pg. 92 & 93
4. A	Chpt. 9, Tbl.5	pg. 718
	Chpt. 9, Tbl. 4	pg. 712

250 kcmil THWN – 0.3970 sq. in. x 1 = 0.3970 sq. in.
400 kcmil THWN – 0.5863 sq. in. x 3 = <u>1.7589 sq. in.</u>
Total = 2.1559 sq. in.

*NOTE: A trade size 3 in. FMC with a permitted fill area of 2.827 sq. in. @ 40% fill should be selected.

5. D	517.18(A)&(B)	pg. 444
6. B	250.24(C)(1)	pg. 105
	Tbl. 250.66	pg. 115
7. C	210.19(A)(1)	pg. 52
	210.11(A)	pg. 51

400 kVA x 1,000 = 400,000 VA
400,000 VA x 125% (continuous load) = 500,000 VA (bldg.)

120 volts x 20 amperes = 5,540 VA (one circuit)

<u>500,000 VA (bldg. lighting)</u> = 90.2 = 91 lighting circuits
   5,540 VA (one circuit)

*NOTE: Circuits need only to be installed to serve the connected load.

8. B	404.8(B)	pg. 268
9. B	240.83(C)	pg. 97
10. D	517.13(B),Ex.2	pg. 443

Copyright© 2016

11. C   680.23(B)(2)(b)   pg. 581

12. B   445.13   pg. 347

13. B   502.10(A)(1)(4)   pg. 386

14. B   Tbl. 514.3(B)(1)   pg. 427

15. C   695.14(D)   pg. 620

16. C   Tbl. 310.15(B)(16)   pg. 154
              Tbl. 310.15(B)(2)(a)   pg. 150
              Tbl. 310.15(B)(3)(a)   pg. 152

    Size 750 kcmil AL ampacity (before derating) = 435 amperes
    435 amps x 1.04 (temp. corrrection) x .8 (adjustment factor) = 361.92 amperes

17. C   392.18(D)&(E)   pg. 240

18. C   324.10(A)   pg. 189

19. C   Single-Phase Current Formula
              Tbl. 310.15(B)(16)   pg. 154

    I = P ÷ E I = 23,600 VA ÷ 240 volts = 98.33 amperes
  *NOTE: Size 1 AWG AL USE cable with an ampacity of 100 amperes should
       be selected.

20. A   220.43(B)   pg. 64

21. D   Tbl. 220.42   pg. 64

    Total lighting equals 205,400 VA
    1st. 3000 VA @ 100 %   = 3,000 VA
    next 117,000 VA @ 35%   = 40,950 VA
    remainder [205.4 kVA - 120 kVA] = 85,400 VA @ 25%   = <u>21,350 VA</u>
                            Total demand = 65,300 VA

22. A   Chpt. 9, Tbl. 5   pg. 717 & 718
              Chpt. 9, Tbl. 4   pg. 712

    Size 10 AWG THHW = .0243 sq. in. x 24 = 0.5832 sq. in.
    Size 10 AWG THHN = .0211 sq. in. x 10 = 0.2110 sq. in.
    Size 12 AWG THHN = .0133 sq. in. x 14 = <u>0.1865 sq. in.</u>
                        Total = 0.9807 sq. in.

  *Note: 2 in. EMT with a 40% allowable fill of 1.342 sq. in. should be selected.

23. A   Tbl. 220.54   pg. 65

   Demand = 35% minus .5% for each dryer exceeding
   23 40 dryers − 23 = 17 (exceeding 23) x .5% = 8.5%
   35% − 8.5% = 26.5% demand

   40 dryers x 6 kW = 240 kW x 26.5% (demand) = 63.6 kW 63.6 kW x 1000 = 63,600 watts
   I = P ÷ E   I = 63,600 watts ÷ 240 volts = 265 amperes

24. D   440.22(A)   pg. 343

25. D   220.14(H)(2)   pg. 63
                    645.5(A)   pg. 561
                    210.19(A)(1)   pg. 52

   90 ft. x 180 VA per ft. x 125% = 20,250 VA (multioutlet assembly)

   20 amps x 120 volts = 2,400 VA (one circuit)

   $\dfrac{20{,}250 \text{ VA (total load)}}{2{,}400 \text{ VA (one circuit)}}$ = 8.43 = 9 circuits

##

MASTER ELECTRICIAN
PRACTICE EXAM #15
ANSWER KEY

ANSWER	REFERENCE	NEC PG.#
1. D	760.43	pg. 652 & 653
2. C	Chpt. 9, Tbl. 1	pg. 711
3. A	700.12	pg. 624
4. C	517.71(A),Ex.	pg. 455
5. A	620.61(B)(1)	pg. 542
6. C	Tbl. 300.50	pg. 146
7. C	551.71	pg. 500
8. A	430.6 & 6(A)(1)	pg. 311
	Tbl. 430.250	pg. 338
	430.22	pg. 316
	Tbl. 400.5(A)(1),Col.A	pg. 258

FLC of motor = 52 amperes x 125% = 65 amperes

*NOTE: Size 2 AWG SO cord with an ampacity of 80 amperes should be selected.

9. B	Tbl. 430.250	pg. 338

63 amperes x 1.1 (power factor) = 69.3 amperes

10. D	682.11	pg. 591
11. D	700.12(F)	pg. 625 & 626
12. C	368.17(B),Ex.	pg. 225
13. B	Tbl. 310.15(B)(16)	pg. 154
	240.4(B)(3)	pg. 90
	240.6(A)	pg. 91

Size 4/0 AWG AL conductors rated @ 75 deg. C ampacity = 180 amperes Next standard size OCP is rated at 200 amperes.

*NOTE: Sec. 240.4(F) requires secondary OCP on delta-wye transformers.

14. C   332.24(1)   pg. 195

15. C   322.10(3)   pg. 188

16. A   Tbl. 300.5   pg. 138

17. A   430.6(A)(2)   pg. 312
                 430.32(A)(1)   pg. 319

   FLA of motor = 18 amps x 115% = 20.7 amperes

18. D   430.32(C)   pg. 320

   FLA of motor = 18 amps x 130% = 23.4 amperes

19. B   450.3(B)   pg. 348
                 Tbl. 450.3(B)   pg. 349
                 240.6(A)   pg. 91

   $I = \dfrac{kVA \times 1{,}000}{E \times 1.732} = \dfrac{50 \times 1{,}000}{480 \times 1.732} = \dfrac{50{,}000 \text{ VA}}{831.36} = 60.2$ amperes

   60.2 amperes x 250% = 150.5 amperes

20. A   220.14(I)   pg. 63
                 220.44   pg. 64
                 Tbl. 220.44   pg. 64

   150 receptacles x 180 VA = 27,000 VA
   1st. 10,000 VA @ 100%   = 10,000 VA
   (remainder) 17,000 VA @ 50%   = 8,500 VA
               TOTAL DEMAND = 18,500 VA

21. A   314.16(B)(4)   pg. 178
                 Tbl. 314.16(A)   pg. 179

   [masonry box] 9 (Size 12 AWG conductors permitted per gang)
            2 conductors (switch)
        7 wires per box x 3 gang = 21 conductors

22. C   502.15(2)   pg. 387

23. D   800.25   pg. 670

24. A   547.5(F)   pg. 479

25. C   450.13(B)   pg. 352
###

Copyright© 2016

MASTER ELECTRICIAN
PRACTICE EXAM #16
ANSWER KEY

ANSWER	REFERENCE	NEC PG.#
1. A	502.130(A)(3)	pg. 389
2. D	Trade Knowledge	
3. C	760.130(B)(2)	pg. 655
4. A	Tbl. 210.21(B)(3)	pg. 54
5. C	450.9	pg. 352
6. B	250.24(A)	pg. 104
7. A	Tbl. 680.8	pg. 578
8. C	Tbl. 310.15(B)(16)	pg. 154
	Tbl. 310.15(B)(2)(a)	pg. 150
	Tbl. 310.15(B)(3)(a)	pg. 152

$$\frac{200 \text{ amperes (load)}}{.75 \text{ (temp. cor.)} \times .8 \text{ (adj. factor)}} = \frac{200}{.6} = 333 \text{ amperes}$$

*NOTE: Size 400 kcmil conductors with an ampacity of 335 amperes should be selected.

9. C	314.16(B)(1)&(5)	pg. 178
	Tbl. 314.16(B)	pg. 179

6 AWG ungrounded conductors	- 3 x 5.00 cu. in.	= 15.00 cu. in.
6 AWG grounded conductors	- 3 x 5.00 cu. in.	= 15.00 cu. in.
8 AWG grounding conductor	- 1 x 3.00 cu. in.	= 3.00 cu. in.
12 AWG ungrounded conductors	- 3 x 2.25 cu. in.	= 6.75 cu. in.
12 AWG grounded conductors	- 3 x 2.25 cu. in.	= 6.75 cu. in.
12 AWG grounding conductor	- 1 x -0- cu. in.	= -0- cu. in.
	TOTAL	= 46.50 cu. in.

10. B	680.21(A)(3)	pg. 579
11. A	700.12(B)(2)	pg. 625
12. C	511.7(B)(1)(b)	pg. 421

Copyright© 2016

13. C	430.6(A)(1)	pg. 311
	Tbl. 430.250	pg. 338
	Tbl. 430.52	pg. 332

FLC of 10 hp motor = 30.8 amperes x 250% = 77 amperes

14. D	610.14(E)(3)	pg. 528
	Tbl. 610.14(E)	pg. 530
15. B	690.64	pg. 605
	705.12(D)(2)	pg. 632
16. A	501.15(C)(6)	pg. 379
17. C	230.42(B)	pg. 82
	Tbl. 310.15(B)(7)	pg. 153
18. C	445.12(B)	pg. 347
19. C	430.6(A)(1)	pg. 311
	Tbl. 430.250	pg. 338
	430.52(C)(1),Ex.2(c)	pg. 322
	240.6(A)	pg. 91

FLC of 50 hp motor = 65 amperes x 400% = 260 amperes

20. D	250.30(A)	pg. 106
21. A	517.32(H)	pg. 448
22. A	504.10(A)	pg. 395
23. B	250.24(C)(3)	pg. 105
24. A	3-phase Current Formula	

$$I = \frac{kVA \times 1{,}000}{E \times 1.732} = \frac{150 \times 1{,}000}{480 \times 1.732} = \frac{150{,}000}{831.36} = 180.32 \text{ amperes}$$

25. C	Tbl. 300.5, Col. 1	pg. 138

###

SIGN ELECTRICIAN
PRACTICE EXAM #17
ANSWER KEY

ANSWER	REFERENCE	NEC PG.#
1. B	300.5(B) 310.10(B)&(C)(2)	pg. 137 pg. 147 & 148
2. A	250.118(2),(3)&(4)	pg. 122
3. B	300.14	pg. 142
4. B	210.19(A)(1),IN#4	pg. 53

120 volts x 3% = 3.6 volts

5. B	Trade Knowledge	
6. D	600.32(A)(5)	pg. 523
7. D	Tbl. 300.5, Col. 2	pg. 138
8. A	250.119 200.6(A)&(B)	pg. 123 pg. 46
9. B	Trade Knowledge	
10. D	600.31(B)	pg. 523
11. B	ANNEX C, Tbl. C.10	pg. 792
12. C	310.110(A),(B)&(C) 250.119 200.7(A)(1)	pg. 172 pg. 123 pg. 47
13. A	600.3(A)	pg. 519
14. C	600.9(A)	pg. 521
15. B	600.5(B)(2)	pg. 519
16. A	250.8(A)	pg. 103
17. A	410.138	pg. 288

Copyright© 2016

18. B	410.68	pg. 285
19. A	310.106(C)	pg. 172
20. B	600.6(B)	pg. 520
21. D	600.5(B)	pg. 519
	210.19(A)(1)	pg. 52
22. B	600.9(C)	pg. 521
23. B	Tbl. 310.15(B)(16)	pg. 154
24. B	600.5(A)	pg. 579
25. D	600.6(A)(1)	pg. 520
	Art. 100	pg. 29

##

SIGN ELECTRICIAN
PRACTICE EXAM #18
ANSWER KEY

ANSWER	REFERENCE	NEC PG.#
1. B	600.21(E)	pg. 522
2. D	600.10(C)(2)	pg. 522
3. A	Trade Knowledge	
4. A	680.57(C)(2)	pg. 589
5. B	680.57(A)&(B)	pg. 589
6. C	110.9	pg. 35
7. C	Tbl. 314.16(B)	pg. 179
	Tbl. 314.16(A)	pg. 179

size 12 AWG = 2.25 cu. in. x 2 = 4.5 cubic inches
size 8 AWG = 3.00 cu. in. x 3 = 9.0 cubic inches
                TOTAL = 13.5 cubic inches

8. C	600.10(D)(2)	pg. 522
9. C	240.4(D)(7)	pg. 90
10. A	600.7(B)(7)(1)	pg. 521
11. D	600.8(C)	pg. 521
12. D	348.12(1)	pg. 205
13. A	352.30(A)	pg. 209
14. C	352.26	pg. 209
15. C	600.5(B)(1)	pg. 519
16. B	225.25(2)	pg. 73

Copyright© 2016

17. A	600.5(C)(3)	pg. 520
	410.30(B)(1)	pg. 282
18. B	225.11	pg. 72
	230.52	pg. 83
19. B	Tbl. 352.44	pg. 210

3.65 in. (per hundred feet) x 2 = 7.3 inches

20. B	600.32(J)(1)	pg. 524
21. C	230.79(D)	pg. 85
22. A	Trade Knowledge	
23. C	Trade Knowledge	
24. B	225.6(A)(1)	pg. 71
25. A	Fig. 514.3	pg. 428

##

RESIDENTIAL ELECTRICIANS
FINAL EXAM
ANSWER KEY

ANSWER	REFERENCE	NEC PG.#
1. B	550.32(F)	pg. 490
2. D	314.17(C)	pg. 180
3. C	422.11(E)(3)	pg. 291
	240.6(A)	pg. 91
	Current Formula	

$$I = \frac{VA}{volts} \quad I = \frac{3{,}600}{240} = 15 \text{ amperes} \times 150\% = 22.5 \text{ amperes}$$

*NOTE: The next standard size circuit breaker with a rating of 25 amperes should be selected.

4. B	Tbl. 220.55 & Note 4	pg. 66
	334.80	pg. 198
	Tbl. 310.15(B)(16)	pg. 154
	Current Formula	

17 kW - 12 kW = 5 kW × 5% = 25% (increase in Col. C)
8 kW (one appliance, Col. C) × 1.25 = 10 kW demand

$$I = \frac{power}{volts} \quad I = \frac{10 \text{ kW} \times 1{,}000}{240 \text{ volts}} = \frac{10{,}000}{240} = 41.66 \text{ amperes}$$

*NOTE: Size 6 AWG NM cable with an ampacity of 55 amperes should be selected.

5. A	550.32(C)	pg. 489
6. A	314.23(B)(1)	pg. 180
7. D	334.104	pg. 198
8. C	314.16(B)(4)	pg. 178

Copyright © 2016

9.	D	406.12,Ex.3	pg. 274
10.	A	334.80	pg. 198
11.	B	210.19(A)(3)	pg. 53
12.	C	210.8(A)(3)	pg. 50
13.	A	680.22(C)	pg. 580
14.	D	Art. 100 Def.	pg. 26
15.	D	440.64	pg. 346
16.	C	210.52(E)(1)	pg. 57
17.	B	300.5(D)(3)	pg. 139
18.	A	200.7(C)(1)	pg. 47
19.	A	250.24(A)	pg. 104
20.	A	220.51	pg. 64
21.	B	590.4(D)(1) 590.6(A)	pg. 517 pg. 518
22.	D	210.70(A)(1),Ex.#2	pg. 58
23.	D	210.8(A)(3),Ex.	pg. 50
24.	B	314.17(C),Ex.	pg. 180
25.	D	Tbl. 310.15(B)(7)	pg. 153
26.	C	334.112	pg. 198
27.	A	Tbl. 300.5, Col.5	pg. 138
28.	C	550.10(D)	pg. 482
29.	D	410.117(C) 348.20(A)(2)c.	pg. 286 pg. 206
30.	A	440.62(B)	pg. 346
31.	B	410.10(D)	pg. 281
32.	B	300.4(B)(1)	pg. 136

33. C	411.4(B)	pg. 290
34. D	250.53(A)(2)	pg. 112
	250.53(D)(2)	pg. 113
35. B	240.6(A)	pg. 91
36. B	250.53(G)	pg. 113
37. A	680.42	pg. 586
	680.22(A)(3)	pg. 579
38. C	210.63	pg. 58
	210.70(A)(3)	pg. 58
39. A	210.11(C)(1),(2)&(3)	pg. 52
40. A	220.53	pg. 65

4800 VA + 1200 VA + 1150 VA + 800 VA + 1200 VA = 9150 VA TOTAL
9150 VA x 75% (demand) = 6862.5 VA

41. D	240.4(D)(7)	pg. 90
42. C	Tbl. 310.15(B)(7)	pg. 153
43. A	424.3(B)	pg. 296
	210.19(A)(1)	pg. 52

20 amps / 125% = 16 amps OR 20 amps x 80% = 16 amperes

44. C	210.63	pg. 58
45. B	680.21(A)(1)	pg. 579
46. D	210.52(G)(1)	pg. 58
47. C	250.66	pg. 115
	Tbl. 250.66	pg. 115
48. A	250.24(C)(1)	pg. 105
49. A	210.52(4)	pg. 55
50. A	210.52(H)	pg. 58
51. D	Tbl. 210.21(B)(2)	pg. 54
52. B	550.32(A)	pg. 489
53. C	406.12,Ex.(1)	pg. 273

54. A	410.116(B)	pg. 286
55. D	250.52(A)(3)(2)	pg. 112
56. C	210.52(I)	pg. 58
57. D	110.6	pg. 35
58. B	334.15(B)	pg. 197
59. A	110.12	pg. 35
60. C	406.9(B)(1)	pg. 272
61. C	690.31(A)	pg. 601
62. D	240.24(E)	pg. 95
63. A	314.21	pg. 180
64. D	680.22(A)(4)	pg. 579
65. C	230.79(C)	pg. 85
66. B	210.52(C)(2)	pg. 56
67. D	210.52(E)(3)	pg. 57
68. A	Current formula	
	422.11(E)(3)	pg. 291
	240.6(A)	pg. 91

$I = P \div E$ $I = 5000 \text{ watts} \div 240 \text{ volts} = 20.8 \text{ amperes}$
20.8 amperes x 150% = 31.24 amperes
*NOTE: The next standard size circuit breaker with a rating of 35 amperes should be selected.

69. B	210.19(A)(3),Ex.1	pg. 53
70. C	210.52(D)	pg. 57
71. D	200.7(C)(1)	pg. 47
72. A	210.52(A)(3)	pg. 56
73. B	300.4(A)(1)	pg. 136
74. B	Tbl. 300.5, Col. 4	pg. 138
75. C	411.2	pg. 289 & 290

##

JOURNEYMAN ELECTRICIAN
FINAL EXAM
ANSWER KEY

ANSWER	REFERENCE	NEC PG.#
1. D	230.24(B)(4)	pg. 80
2. C	200.7(A)(2)	pg. 47
3. A	360.10(1)&(3)	pg. 219
	360.12(1)	pg. 219
4. A	500.5(B)(1)IN#2(5)	pg. 370
5. C	514.9(A)	pg. 428
6. B	Trade Knowledge	
7. D	Single-Phase Current Formula	

$$I = \frac{Power}{volts} \qquad I = \frac{15 \text{ kW} \times 1{,}000}{240 \text{ volts}} = \frac{15{,}000}{240} = 72.1 \text{ amperes}$$

8. C	410.153	pg. 289
9. D	314.16(B)	pg. 178
	314.16(B)(1),(2)&(5)	pg. 178
	Tbl. 314.16(B)	pg. 179

```
2 - 6 AWG ungrounded conductors  = 2 x 5.00 cu. in. = 10 cu. in.
1 - 6 AWG grounded conductor     = 1 x 5.00 cu. in. =  5 cu. in.
1 - 8 AWG equipt. grounding      = 1 x 3.00 cu. in. =  3 cu. in.
2 - internal clamps              = 1 x 5.00 cu. in. =  5 cu. in.
1 - pigtail                      =      -0-         =  0 cu. in.
                                         TOTAL      = 23 cu. in.
```

10. B	445.14	pg. 347
11. B	517.30(C)(3)(1)	pg. 447
12. A	682.11	pg. 591

Copyright© 2016

13. C   424.3(B)   pg. 296
                   210.19(A)(1)   pg. 52
                   Tbl. 310.15(B)(16)   pg. 154

[125 amperes + 2.5 amperes] x 125% = 159 amperes

*NOTE: Size 2/0 AWG conductors with an allowable ampacity of 175 amperes should be selected.

14. D   Tbl. 430.248   pg. 337
                   430.32(A)(2)   pg. 319

15. D   300.6(A)   pg. 139 & 140

16. D   517.18(A)   pg. 444

17. B   605.8(C)   pg. 527

18. A   230.23(B)   pg. 80

19. C   680.43(E)(3)   pg. 587

20. A   344.30(A)   pg. 204

21. C   430.110(A)   pg. 332

22. D   455.9   pg. 356

23. C   430.72(B)(2)   pg. 326
                   Tbl. 430.72, Col. B   pg. 327

24. D   300.9   pg. 140 & 141

25. C   445.12(C)   pg. 347

26. B   430.32(A)(1)   pg. 319

27. B   240.5(B)(4)   pg. 91

28. B   Tbl. 310.15(B)(16)   pg. 154
                   Tbl. 310.15(B)(3)(a)   pg. 152

Size 10 AWG THHN ampacity (before derating) = 40 amperes 40 amps x 50% (adjustment factor for 20 wires) = 20 amperes

29. D   348.12(1)   pg. 205

30. D   250.178   pg. 129

31. C   410.310(G)(1)(2)&(3)   pg. 287

Copyright© 2016

32. D	725.48(B)(1)	pg. 643
	300.3(C)(1)	pg. 136
33. B	Art. 100	pg. 28
34. C	Tbl. 430.250	pg. 338
	430.24(1)	pg. 318

10 hp - FLC = 30.8 amps x 125% = 38.5 amperes
7½ hp - FLC = 24.2 amps x 100% = <u>24.2 amperes</u>
TOTAL = 62.7 amperes

35. B	300.20(A)	pg. 144
36. A	410.68	pg. 285
	Tbl. 310.104(A)	pg. 169
37. D	800.53	pg. 672
38. B	410.62(C)(1)(2)a.	pg. 284
39. C	430.81(B)	pg. 327
40. A	680.26(B)(2)	pg. 584
41. A	110.26(E)(1)(b)	pg. 39
42. C	680.41	pg. 586
43. D	553.7(B)	pg. 512
44. B	Fig. 516.3(C)(1)	pg. 435
45. C	555.17(B)	pg. 515
46. D	Tbl. 430.22(E)	pg. 317
47. A	370.3	pg. 227
48. C	690.47(C)(1)	pg. 604
49. D	518.1	pg. 458
50. C	Tbl. 310.15(B)(16)	pg. 154
	Tbl. 310.15(B)(2)(a)	pg. 150

$\dfrac{200 \text{ amperes (load)}}{.75 \text{ (temp. correction)}}$ = 266.6 amperes

*NOTE: Size 300 kcmil conductors with an allowable ampacity of 285 amperes should be selected.

51. A	Tbl. 300.5, Note 2	pg. 139
52. C	800.44(A)(4)	pg. 671
53. D	362.30(A)	pg. 221
54. B	400.22 & 22(F)	pg. 261
55. A	225.27	pg. 74
56. B	250.190(C)(1)	pg. 131
57. B	Chpt. 9, Tbl. 4 Chpt. 9, Tbl. 5 Note 7 to Chpt. 9 Tbls.	pg. 718 pg. 712 pg. 711

$$\frac{0.897 \text{ sq. in. (conduit)}}{0.0824 \text{ sq. in. (wire)}} = 10.8 = 11 \text{ wires}$$

58. D	Tbl. 310.15(B)(16)	pg. 154
59. D	410.136(B)	pg. 288
60. C	334.116(B)	pg. 198
61. B	400.31(A)	pg. 261
62. D	Tbl. 310.104(A)	pg. 168
63. C	240.21(B)(2)(1)	pg. 93

800 amperes ÷ 3 = 266.6 amperes
*NOTE: Size 300 kcmil THW conductors with an allowable ampacity of 285 amperes should be selected.

64. A	422.12	pg. 292
65. A	220.84(C)(3)(a) Tbl. 220.84	pg. 69 pg. 69

8 kW x 12 = 96 kW x 41% (demand) = 39.36 kW

66. D	645.4(5)	pg. 561
67. C	505.7(A)	pg. 401
68. B	520.41(A)	pg. 462
69. D	314.16(B)(4)	pg. 178
70. A	727.8	pg. 651

71. A	320.10(1)	pg. 186
	320.12(1)&(5)	pg. 186
72. B	334.12(B)(4)	pg. 197
73. C	300.4(E)	pg. 137
74. D	Art. 100	pg. 30
75. C	Tbl. 310.15(B)(16)	pg. 154
	Tbl. 310.15(B)(3)(c)	pg. 152
	Tbl. 310.15(B)(2)(a)	pg. 150

```
  86 deg. F (ambient temp.)
 +40 deg. F (temp adder)
 126 deg. F (derating temp.)
```

500 kcmil CU 75º C rated ampacity = 380 amperes (before derating)
380 amperes x .67 (temp. correction) = 254.6 amperes

76. A	336.104	pg. 199
77. D	408.36,Ex.3	pg. 276
78. A	430.83(A)(1)	pg. 328
79. B	430.40	pg. 321
80. C	690.2	pg. 594
	705.2	pg. 632

###

MASTER ELECTRICIAN
FINAL EXAM
ANSWER KEY

ANSWER	REFERENCE	NEC PG.#
1. D	300.5(B)	pg. 137
	Tbl. 310.104(A)	pg. 169
	Tbl. 310.15(B)(16)	pg. 154
	Current Formula	

I = P ÷ E   I = 90,000 VA ÷ 240 volts = 375 amperes

*NOTE: Size 500 kcmil THHN/THWN conductors with an ampacity of 380 amperes should be selected.

2. B   3-phase Power Formula
                 VA = I x E x 1.732

VA = 416 amperes x 208 volts x 1.732 = 149,866 VA
149,866 VA ÷ 1,000 = 149.8 kVA

3. D	110.75(D)	pg. 45
4. D	645.5(A)	pg. 561
5. D	430.6(A)(2)	pg. 312
	430.32(A)(1)	pg. 319
	430.32(C)	pg. 320

19 amperes x 140% = 26.60 amperes

6. B	517.17(B)	pg. 443
7. C	700.12(A)	pg. 624

120 volts x 87.5% = 105 volts

8. B	430.6(A)(2)	pg. 312
	430.32(C)	pg. 320

54 amperes x 130% = 70.2 amperes

Copyright© 2016

9.	C	500.6(B)(1)	pg. 372
10.	D	392.60(B)(1)&(3)	pg. 245
11.	C	342.28	pg. 202
12.	A	700.12(B)(3),Ex.	pg. 625
13.	B	Tbl. 110.28	pg. 41
14.	C	354.20(B)	pg. 213
15.	D	680.43(B)(1)(a)	pg. 587
16.	A	324.10(B)(2)	pg. 189
17.	C	695.5(B)	pg. 618
18.	B	310.15(B)(5)(a)&(c)	pg. 152
19.	D	250.68(A),Ex.1&2	pg. 115 & 116
20.	D	547.8(C)	pg. 479
21.	B	240.8	pg. 91
22.	A	210.4(B)	pg. 48
23.	D	550.31(1)	pg. 489
24.	D	250.53(A)(2) 250.52(A)(2)-(A)(8)	pg. 112 pg. 111 & 112
25.	A	501.10(B)(2)(2) 502.10(A)(2)	pg. 377 pg. 386
26.	A	525.10(A)	pg. 470
27.	D	382.15(A)	pg. 234
28.	D	230.2(A),(B),&(C)	pg. 79
29.	B	210.8(A)(2)	pg. 50
30.	B	300.22(B)	pg. 144
31.	D	680.21(C)	pg. 579

32. C   424.3(B)   pg. 296
                            210.19(A)(1)   pg. 52
                            Single-Phase Current Formula

$$I = \frac{kW \times 1{,}000}{volts} \quad I = \frac{15 \times 1{,}000}{240} = \frac{15{,}000}{240} = 62.5 \text{ amperes (heater)}$$

     62.5 amperes (heater)
+ 10.0 amperes (blower)
     72.5 amperes x 125% = 91 amperes

33. A   220.56   pg. 65
                            Tbl. 220.56   pg. 67

    14.00 kW - range
     5.00 kW - water heater
     0.75 kW - mixer
     2.50 kW - dishwasher
     2.00 kW - booster heater
     2.00 kW - broiler
   26.25 kW - total connected load x 65% = 17.06 kW

*NOTE: However the NEC® states the demand shall not be less than the two largest pieces of equipment. 14.00 kW + 5.00 kW = 19 kW demand

34. B   250.66(A)   pg. 115

35. B   3-phase current formula
                            Tbl. 310.15(B)(16)   pg. 154

$$I = \frac{54{,}000 \text{ VA}}{208 \times 1.732} = \frac{54{,}000}{360.25} = 149.89 \text{ amperes}$$

*NOTE: Size 1/0 THWN conductors with an ampacity of 150 amperes should be selected.

36. D   Tbl. 630.11(A)   pg. 552
                            630.11(B)   pg. 552

60 amperes x .71 = 43 amperes x 100% = 43 amperes
60 amperes x .71 = 43 amperes x 100% = 43 amperes
50 amperes x .71 = 36 amperes x   85% = 31 amperes
50 amperes x .71 = 36 amperes x   70% = 25 amperes
40 amperes x .71 = 28 amperes x   60% = 17 amperes
40 amperes x .71 = 28 amperes x   60% = <u>17 amperes</u>
                                       TOTAL   = 176 amperes

37. D   480.9(A)   pg. 360

38. C   3-phase Power Formula
$$P = I \times E \times 1.732$$

$$P = 600 \text{ amperes} \times 208 \text{ volts} \times 1.732 \times 80\% = 172{,}923 \text{ VA}$$

39. B   3-phase Current Formula
450.3(B)	pg. 348
Tbl. 450.3(B)	pg. 349
240.6(A)	pg. 91

(Primary)

$$I = \frac{kVA \times 1{,}000}{E \times 1.732} \quad I = \frac{150 \times 1{,}000}{480 \times 1.732} = \frac{150{,}000}{831.36} = 180 \text{ amps} \times 250\% = 450 \text{ amps}$$

(Secondary)

$$I = \frac{kVA \times 1{,}000}{E \times 1.732} \quad I = \frac{150 \times 1{,}000}{208 \times 1.732} = \frac{150{,}000}{360.25} = 416 \text{ amps} \times 125\% = 520 \text{ amps}$$

*NOTE: For the secondary you are permitted to go up to the next standard size overcurrent device which has a rating of 600 amperes.

40. C   645.3   pg. 560
                               300.21   pg. 144

41. B   Tbl. 300.5   pg. 138

42. C   230.7, Ex.1&2   pg. 79

43. A   250.64(A)   pg. 113

44. B   3-phase Current Formula
445.13	pg. 347
Tbl. 310.15(B)(16)	pg. 154

$$I = \frac{kW \times 1{,}000}{\text{volts} \times 1.732} \quad I = \frac{200 \times 1{,}000}{480 \times 1.732} = \frac{200{,}000}{831.36} = 240.56 \text{ amperes (FLC)}$$

241 amperes × 115% = 277 amperes (required ampacity of conductors)

*NOTE: Size 300 kcmil THWN conductors with an allowable ampacity of 285 amperes should be selected.

45. C   502.115(B)   pg. 388

46. D   645.5(B)(1)   pg. 561

47. B   501.15(C)(3)   pg. 379

48. A   220.12   pg. 61
               Tbl. 220.12   pg. 63
               220.52(A)&(B)   pg. 65
               Tbl. 220.42   pg. 64

   4,000 sq. ft. + 2,000 sq. ft. = 6,000 sq. ft. x 3 VA = 18,000 VA
   three small appliance circuits @ 1,500 VA each   = 4,500 VA
   one laundry circuit @ 1,500 VA   = 1,500 VA
                        Total connected load   = 24,000 VA

   1st 3,000 VA @ 100%   3,000 VA
   24,000 VA - 3,000 VA = 21,000 VA (remainder) @ 35% =   7,350 VA
                        Total demand load   =   10,350 VA

49. A   430.6 & .6(A)(1)   pg. 311
               430.22   pg. 316
               Tbl. 430.250   pg. 338
               Tbl. 400.5(A)(1),Col.A   pg. 258

   FLC of 30 HP motor = 40 amperes x 125% = 50 amperes

   *NOTE: Size 4 AWG SOW cord with an allowable ampacity of 60 amperes should
          be selected.

50. B   525.5(B)(2)   pg. 470

51. D   400.8(4),Ex.   pg. 260
               368.56(B)(2)   pg. 225 & 226

52. B   225.6(A)(1)   pg. 71

53. A   430.2   pg. 311

54. C   409.106   pg. 279
               Tbl. 430.97   pg. 330

55. D   210.18   pg. 52
               210.12(A)   pg. 52

56. D   680.9   pg. 577

57. B   700.5(A)   pg. 623
               701.5(A)   pg. 628

58. B   338.10(B)(4)(b)   pg. 200

59. C   314.28(E)   pg. 183 & 184

60. D   390.8   pg. 239

61. A   Tbl. 110.26(A)(1),Cond.3 pg. 38

62. A
550.30 & .31(1) pg. 489
Tbl. 550.31 pg. 489
Single-phase current formula

25 lots x 16,000 VA (minimum) = 400,000 VA
                                X .24   (demand factor)
                               96,000 VA (demand load)

$I = \frac{power}{Volts}$ $I = \frac{96,000 \text{ VA}}{240 \text{ volts}} = 400$ amperes

63. C
3-phase current formula

$I = \frac{kVA \times 1000}{E \times 1.732}$ $I = \frac{150 \times 1000}{208 \times 1.732} = \frac{150,000}{360.25}$ = 416 amperes (FLA)
                                                     - 212 amperes (existing load)
                                                     = 204 amperes (additional load)

64. A 250.146(D) pg. 127
65. D 422.15(C) pg. 292
66. C 800.113(B)(1) pg. 675
67. D 600.6 pg. 520
68. C 368.17(B),Ex. pg. 225
69. C 424.44(A) pg. 299
70. B 408.36,Ex.2 pg. 276
71. D 682.11 pg. 591
72. B 517.35(A) pg. 449
73. D 410.97 pg. 285
74. A 410.54(C) pg. 283
75. D 285.28 pg. 134
       250.64(E) pg. 114
76. C 250.52(A)(2)(1) pg. 111
77. D 520.25(C) pg. 461
78. C 210.62 pg. 58
79. A 503.130(A) pg. 393

Copyright© 2016

80. D	430.22(E) Tbl. 430.22(E)	pg. 316 pg. 317
81. C	604.7 330.30(C)	pg. 526 pg. 194
82. C	517.30(E)	pg. 447
83. D	Tbl. 310.15(B)(16) 240.4(B)(2)&(3) 240.6(A)	pg. 154 pg. 90 pg. 91
84. D	514.11(A)	pg. 428
85. B	Tbl. 110.26(A)(1)	pg. 38
86. B	Tbl. 250.122	pg. 125
87. A	450.11	pg. 352
88. C	388.70	pg. 238
89. A	500.8(E)(2)	pg. 375
90. C	450.21(A)	pg. 352
91. D	Tbl. 680.8	pg. 578
92. D	Tbl. 220.42	pg. 64

205.4 kVA x 1,000 = 205,400 VA

first 3,000 VA @ 100% = 3,000 VA
3,001 to 120,000 VA @ 35% = 117,000 VA @ 35% = 40,950 VA
Remainder 205,400 VA − 120,000 VA = 85,400 VA @ 25% = 21,350 VA
Demand = 65,300 VA

$\frac{65,300 \text{ VA}}{1,000}$ = 65.3 kVA

93. B	694.62	pg. 614
94. A	422.13	pg. 292
95. C	Single-phase current formula Tbl. 310.15(B)(16) Tbl. 310.15(B)(2)(a)	 pg. 154 pg. 150

$I = \frac{\text{power}}{\text{volts}}$ $I = \frac{36,000 \text{ VA}}{240 \text{ volts}}$ = 150 amperes load

required ampacity = $\frac{150 \text{ amperes}}{.75 \text{ (temp. cor.)}}$ = 200 amperes

96. A	504.80(C)	pg. 397
97. C	Chpt. 9, Tbl. 2	pg. 711
98. A	314.28(A)(2)	pg. 183

3.5 inches (conduit) x 6 = 21 inches

99. B	505.8(G)	pg. 402
100. D	392.20(B)(1)	pg. 241

##

TITLES AVAILABLE BASED ON THE 2011 NEC©

Electricians Exam Book

Electricians Handbook of NEC® Questions

Electricians Practice Calculations Exams

Practical Calculations for Electricians

Copyright© 2016

ELECTRICIANS EXAM BOOK

Based on the 2011 NEC®, this comprehensive self-study guide is specifically designed for licensing exams and National Electrical Code® review. It contains 18 practice exams of 25 questions each, and three final exams of 75 to 100 questions differing in length and difficulty, based upon the examination level. Each exam contains types of questions one will encounter on actual tests to identify your strength and weaknesses. This book covers all topics that are included on most journeyman, master, contractor, inspector, residential, sign, and maintenance licensing exams. Even with limited study time this kind of selective study yields maximum tests results. The text will familiarize you with the exam and enable practice in answer questions involving judgment, evaluation and reasoning. **"Answer key" with NEC® references included.**

8 ½ in. by 11 in. Spiral-bound. 244 pages. ISBN 978-1-935834-04-5
Retail price: $37.95